Puddn'head

PARENTING

Pudd'nhead

PARENTING

Forming a POSITIVE Working Relationship
with a Child with ADD

STERLING B. PRATT

NEW YORK

Pudd'nhead PARENTING
Forming a Positive Working Relationship with a Child with ADD

ISBN 978-1-61448-103-4 paperback
ISBN 978-1-61448-104-1 eBook
Library of Congress Control Number: 2011935647

Morgan James Publishing
The Entrepreneurial Publisher
5 Penn Plaza, 23rd Floor, New York City, New York 10001
(212) 655-5470 office • (516) 908-4496 fax
www.MorganJamesPublishing.com

In an effort to support local communities, raise awareness and funds, Morgan James Publishing donates one percent of all book sales for the life of each book to Habitat for Humanity. Get involved today.

www.HelpHabitatForHumanity.org

To my children, Shelly, Sterling, Christy, Forrest, Mallory, and Jordan, who tolerated my wife and me as we learned from many mistakes at their expense, and who accept the fact that we will never become perfect parents.

To my wife, Terry, and her family who taught me so much about unconditionally loving, supporting, and serving.

To my father, who in spite of his few words taught me integrity and convinced me that I was cherished.

Finally, to my mother who worked so hard to fix me at a time when so little was known about what was broken. She passed on to me her DNA to write and teach, and always told me I was "magnificent" at it.

ACKNOWLEDGEMENTS

This book is one of those great things in life that forces you to ask for and accept the help and support of others. I would first and foremost like to thank my wife, Terry, who insisted I stop talking about writing a book and actually do it. She also supported me every step of the way with constant encouragement and many hours combing through the manuscript to find one more spelling error. The first real editor to see the manuscript was my mother, who taught high school English for several decades and published two grammar text books. The evenings we spent debating our way through the manuscript was both fun and beneficial. I give much credit to my talented niece, Allison Kartchner for her professional editing. She was kind enough to mark the many errors in green instead of red ink so that the volume of corrections was not as alarming. Speaking of talent, I thank my good friend Jennifer Beichner for her professional feedback on the style, organization and tone of the book. You, the reader, are benefitting from her many valuable suggestions. I also received great feedback from several people who agreed to review my early manuscript simply because they wanted to help someone who was trying to help you and your child. In alphabetical order these generous individuals are Beth Kaplanek, Erica Schwartz, Gerri Galiffa, Jodi Sleeper-Triplett, Kim Smith Kidd, Linda Smith, and Laurie Chester. My three wonderful daughters, Shelly, Christy, and Mallory also contributed feedback and encouragement. If you like the beautiful interior layout, you have my sister, Jaye Pratt to thank. I don't have to tell you that she is gifted at what she does. You are holding the proof.

As for the content of this book I have many people who have helped form my understanding of ADD. They are too many to list, but I thank them for their intelligence, research, and dedication, and for their willingness to share it with the world.

Finally, I thank God for the inspiration to write this book and for his guidance during the writing process. As you read this book, if you count me as being talented or insightful those are blessings from whom all blessings come. They came at birth, during my life, or during the writing of this book, but they came from Him. If this book does what I hope; if it helps you have a better relationship with your child and helps you guide them to a happier more fulfilling life, God is the one to thank.

CONTENTS

The Fear
and the Hope

THE FACTS ARE COLD AND HARD

As you start to learn about ADD the statistics can be quite alarming. I'm not referring to the statistics about how many kids have ADD, how many go undiagnosed, or how many are misdiagnosed. Aside from your sympathy toward kids in general, those statistics don't concern you. Your biggest concern, and rightfully so, is your own son or daughter.

Sooner or later you are going to come across alarming statistics about their shaky future. You're going to read that kids with ADD are twice as likely to become addicted to drugs or alcohol and four times more likely to be arrested. In fact, you will hear that our jails are full of people who struggled as kids with ADD. You're going to hear that because your child has ADD they are more likely to experiment at an early age with cigarettes, alcohol, marijuana, prescriptions drugs, and sex. Studies show that they are eight times more likely to be involved in dangerous sex or an unplanned pregnancy. They are also more likely to be involved in violent or dangerous recreation such as fight clubs or base jumping, and destructive behavior such as self-mutilation and even suicide.

> Because your child has ADD, you will be focusing more intently on parenting them the right way, and they will be even more likely to avoid destructive behaviors than the general population.

Unfortunately, from my experience working with and observing kids with ADD and talking with their parents, I feel that the scientific community can confidently stand by those ominous statistics. If you are hearing them for the first time, I understand the panic and fear that may be racing through your mind at this moment as you visualize your child falling into those destructive patterns. Maybe you are in denial, thinking, "Not my child," and you may be right. However, to assume such would be a dangerous game of Russian roulette. It's a gamble I've seen other parents take and later lament.

THE HOPE

That was the bad news. Take it as a wake-up call. Take it as a warning. Use it as a fear-based motivation to take the actions you will learn in this book and to search other valuable sources of sound advice on raising a child with ADD.

This book is about how to beat those odds; how to hedge the bet that your child will have the self-confidence and self-esteem to bypass all of those pitfalls and go on to enjoy a successful and self-fulfilling life. After all, isn't that all we want for them, with all our hearts? Don't we wake up every day and pray that today they will have a good day, that they will not let themselves be worn down by an abrasive world? Aren't we willing to do anything, give anything, and even give up anything to help them overcome their nature and make choices that will lead to a future full of possibilities, opportunities and fulfillment?

As you go through these essential steps for helping your child thrive with ADD, you will find ways to be grateful for their ADD. Here is the first one, and I give it to you in the form of a guarantee:

If you do your best to follow the steps outlined in this book, not only will your child have a better chance of beating the odds for kids with ADD, they will likely defy the odds for kids in general. That's right, because your child has ADD, you will be focusing more intently on parenting them the right way, and they will be even more likely to avoid destructive behaviors than the general population.

I Know What You're Going Through

Before I outline the how, let me tell you the why; why I am so interested in your success as a parent raising a child with ADD. It is because I know what you and your child are going through, and I know that you can succeed. My struggles growing up with ADD make it easy for me to understand and empathize with what your child is experiencing each day. My struggles as a parent of children with ADD make it easy for me to empathize with your daily frustration and your concern for the future. And finally, my success in life has made it easy for me to have hope for both you and your child's success.

Let me give you just a taste of my personal ADD experience.

AS A KID

In my early years I was quiet, spacey, and even-tempered. This may have been what inspired my mom to nickname me Pudd'nhead. She claims that it was simply a term of endearment that held no judgment. If you've read *Pudd'nhead Wilson* by Mark Twain (one of my mother's favorite authors) you may doubt her claim. The townsfolk in Twain's story go through terms like "the downrightest fool in the world," "ain't in his right mind," "hain't got any mind," "lummox," "simon-pure labrick," "dam fool," and "perfect jackass" before settling on Mr. Wilson's permanent nickname, *Pudd'nhead*. See what I mean? My mom's inspiration for my nickname is quite suspicious.

I was a bright child in many ways, as I'm sure your child is. At the age of five I had learned to read by listening in on my five older siblings. As a result, my parents had me tested for readiness to enter first grade a year early. In my mom's words, my scores on the math test were "off the charts." So, equipped with both reading skills and an aptitude for math, I embarked on my fateful scholastic career.

Was I ready for first grade? Judge for yourself. Each time Mrs. Butterfield placed a worksheet on my desk, I filled in my name and answered the first couple of questions, and then drifted off into some wild superhero adventure. My ADD brain had come with a vivid imagination. It was more interesting to indulge in my various daydreams than to prove to my teacher that I already understood the material we were studying.

In the majority of cases ADD comes with one or more coexisting disorders. It was obvious by my first grade experience that mine had come with a social anxiety disorder (SAD). I didn't speak with or otherwise interact with any student in my class. I simply observed both their behavior and emotions. I still remember which kids were popular, which ones worked hard at being popular, which ones were shy, and which ones felt left out.

I remember one tall, skinny girl with short, curly, brown hair who went home often with a stomachache. I sensed that her stomachaches

---

The townsfolk in Twain's story go through terms like "the downrightest fool in the world," "ain't in his right mind," "hain't got any mind," "lummox," "simon-pure labrick," "dam fool," and "perfect jackass" before settling on Mr. Wilson's permanent nickname, Pudd'nhead.

and frequent trips to the restroom were a product of how she felt emotionally. I also noticed that no one else seemed to notice her anxiety.

In spite of my failing grades I was promoted to second grade the following year. I did somewhat better, due to some rudimentary feedback and reward systems my mother and Mrs. McCray devised, involving colored toothpicks and curly ribbon. Nevertheless, I was still removed from the advanced reading group because I had to be nudged each time it was my turn to read. The reading group met at a round table near the windows looking out into the courtyard where I continued my various out-of-body adventures. Reading wasn't a problem; staying focused was.

In third grade I was tortured by Mrs. Davis who didn't understand or accept the weird manifestations of my emerging obsessive-compulsive disorder (OCD). Her favorite discipline method was to entertain the class at my expense. She took it upon herself to break me of running my finger along a mortar joint in the cinder block hallway between our classroom and the cafeteria. She had the class stand in the hallway outside our classroom and watch as I walked to the cafeteria and back, stepping on only the center tiles.

She also interpreted my outside-the-lines approach to some assignments as an open act of rebellion, and reacted by illustrating to the class what happened to such anarchists. On one occasion I was forced to sit in front of the class for an hour holding an art project she felt I had crafted in a subversive style. Subversive style? I was a quiet, spacey seven-year-old without a rebellious bone in my body.

My inability to regulate my emotions sometimes made Mrs. Davis's effort to embarrass me exponentially more effective. In fact, I ended the very last day of that year sitting in front of the class, holding in my lap what she called her "Crying Bucket." I was making good use of it.

In fourth grade, the compassionate and patient Mrs. Farris took great care of me. She sent a note home to my mom after getting the scores from my IQ and equivalency tests. She wanted to reassure her that I had some brains in my head, not just pudding. She thought it would help, but it simply convinced my mom, and then me, that I was just lazy. It also amped up my mom's futile and frustrated efforts to motivate me.

That IQ test crystallized for me the bane of every kid with ADD's school career: the performance-to-potential gap. That gap is the reason behind teacher after teacher uttering the shaming phrase, "You have so much potential; why don't you just apply yourself?" The more beloved the teacher, the more it hurt. The more I applied myself, the more discouraging it was to fall short and disappoint them, and me.

GROWING UP?

By fifth grade I started to spend more and more time in the principal's office. By sixth grade I started fighting. By seventh grade I quit caring about making As. By eighth grade I had become a pretty good liar. And, during my ninth grade year I ran away from home, twice.

In spite of my inability to manage homework assignments and remember to study for tests, I managed to get through high school with a few As, mostly Bs and Cs, a few Ds, and amazingly only one F.

The F was in my ninth grade advanced math class. Toward the end of seventh grade my math teacher, Mrs. Bird, sent me to the lunch room to take the test for the advanced math program. One of the people at my testing table came right out and asked me what I was doing there. The other people at the table thought it was an excellent question. I guess Mrs. Bird had noticed that when I did turn in homework, it was always right. Those same kids were even more surprised when I showed up to Mr. Bishop's algebra class the next year.

Mr. Bishop was excited to see me in his class. He had taught some of my older siblings, and we had several brief conversations about math theory the previous year. Before long he was singing the same depressing dirge as my other teachers: "You could do this stuff in your sleep, why don't you turn in your homework?" My fourth and final semester with him, I had a 95 percent test average and a zero homework average. I felt he was justified in both his disappointment in me and the F.

THE OLE COLLEGE TRY

After high school I took the ACT test and applied for college. The university of my choice replied with the following statement. I am paraphrasing, of course. "Your high school transcript stinks but you scored so high on the ACT test that we are going to take a chance on you."

Despite my enthusiastic and resolute attitude at the start of the first semester, I was soon overwhelmed by the academic and social complexities of college life. The result was a 0.4 GPA. No, I didn't type that backwards—I actually achieved a point four GPA. The university determined that they had taken a bad risk, and in accordance with their policy I was placed on academic probation for the following semester. After an even more dedicated and heroic effort my second semester, they fully repented of their bad gamble and booted me out.

AS AN ADULT

What a hit to my self-esteem! Some kids might have given up after such a devastating failure. However, my resilient spirit survived and after several more attempts at college, and various businesses and careers, I finally found some superpowers; and one of my sweet spots.

I have to credit my mother-in-law, Shirley, for some of those discoveries. I had dropped by her house for lunch one day and was enjoying a plate of her delicious leftovers while watching Gomer Pyle and grumbling about how bored I was working my pest control business. An ad came on the TV for a local technical college, Miller

Institute, which prepared students for an exciting career in computer programming. Shirley suggested that I go enroll. Mostly just to tease and shock her, I immediately jumped up, said something to the effect of, "That's a great idea!", and hurried toward the door. She asked me where I was going, and I replied over my shoulder that I always did everything she told me to do, and that I was of course going to the school right then to enroll. The part of me that wasn't just teasing my mother-in-law was desperate to jump into something new, challenging, and stimulating. So, I jumped into my pest control truck and drove straight across town to Miller Institute to enroll.

The school counselor had me take a pre-enrollment aptitude test. Since test taking itself was one of my superpowers, I aced the test and a couple of weeks later found myself in a fast-paced, technical curriculum that stimulated every neuron in my brain. Three months into their twelve-month program, I had devoured the material and completed all the assignments for the first six months and had started in on the material for the second six months. At four months I was tutoring students who were struggling in month ten and was also hired as a lab aid. After six months I left school, flew to Dallas, and got a job with the most dominant computer programming company at the time, EDS. At EDS I continued to excel in a way that I had never experienced in my life.

I'm not trying to brag, I'm just trying to give you a taste of what your child will experience when they find their superpowers, and their sweet spot. Superpowers are something I will explain in detail later, along with how to help your child find them before their late twenties, like I did. Your child's superpowers will lead them to their sweet spot. Once they arrive there, everything will change. Life will start to flow in their direction. Everything will become more enjoyable and more fulfilling.

The only thing that will stand in their way is a lingering lack of self-esteem. After years of beating myself up for all my inexplicable failures, I had developed some fairly inaccurate perceptions of myself. Recovering my self-esteem was a long drawn-out process of learning and practicing. It is the part of my journey your child will have the chance to avoid, or at least shorten, as a result of you following the steps in this book.

AS A PARENT

My wife and I chose to bring six children into this world and each one holds an equally tender place in our hearts. We watched with excitement as their unique personalities developed and their true natures unfolded. We hurt with their pain and failures and we rejoiced in their successes. Now my wife and I are going through those same emotions watching our children love and care for our grandchildren.

I also hold feelings of affection and empathy for nieces and nephews, the kids I have worked with as a scoutmaster, soccer and basketball coach, and even as a parent helping with my children's field trips and science camps. Because of my own struggles, I always recognized and gravitated toward those kids who were struggling with self-confidence and self-esteem.

I KNOW ABOUT YOUR LOVE

It is human nature to assume that everyone else in the world feels the same way you do. If that assumption is at all true, it tells me that, just like me, you have an amazing amount of love and compassion for your amazing child.

Another reason I assume you love your son or daughter is that you are reading this book. You are taking the time to learn about what is causing them pain and frustration. I'm sure this isn't the first thing you've done to help them be happy and successful in life. I'm sure you have worked and sacrificed many times with that goal

> Your child's superpowers will lead them to their
> sweet spot. Once they arrive there, everything will change.
> Life will start to flow in their direction. Everything will
> become more enjoyable and more fulfilling.

in mind. That work and sacrifice, regardless of its effectiveness, illustrates your love.

I hope you open your mind to the principles I will share with you. I hope you have the faith to try the steps I have outlined in this book. I promise that as you do, your relationship with your son or daughter will become more enjoyable and less frustrating for both of you. You will watch them become a more cooperative partner with you in meeting the challenges of ADD. Both of you will take courage from the progress they make and feel greater hope for their future.

First, a Few Precepts about Parenting

SECTION ONE

Working Right

When it comes to parenting your child, loving them and *work-ing hard* isn't enough. One of my mentors, James Malinchak, who has focused for decades on teaching kids the keys to success, teaches the principle that *working hard* and *working smart* are not enough. Instead, he urges his protégés to *work right*.

WORKING HARD

You need to realize that no matter how loving and pure your motives are, *working hard* will not get you there. In fact, when it comes to helping your child, *working hard* without *working right* will generally do more damage than good. Children will typically react to your increased effort with increased resistance and eventual defiance. All your *hard work* will send a message that they are inept and stupid and the only way to prove otherwise is for them to conquer their ADD challenges without your help.

I see some parents put everything they have into fixing their child with the results of only breaking them more. At some point those parents give in to the feelings of "I'm such a terrible parent." They start to question why they ever had kids in the first place. The truth is they aren't terrible parents. They are wonderful, caring, loving parents who are *working hard* to help their child. They just aren't *working right.*

WORKING SMART

Adele Faber, the coauthor of *How to Talk So Kids Will Listen & Listen So Kids Will Talk* started her book with the following paragraph: "I was a wonderful parent before I had children. I was an expert on why everyone else was having problems with theirs. Then I had three of my own."

In our early parenting, my wife, Terry, and I thought working smart was the way to go. We thought we could think things through, plan things out, make smart decisions, and everything would go well. We were going to do all the things our parents did right, throw out all the things they did wrong, and combine the result with theories from our college psychology classes. We felt well armed and fully loaded with knowledge and wisdom. It wasn't long before our frustrations told us otherwise. We look back now in amazement at how naive and ill prepared we were. We were *working hard* and *working smart,* but not always *working right.*

LEARNING TO WORK RIGHT

Learning from Mistakes

One way to learn to *work right* is to make lots of mistakes and experience pain from your own frustration and from watching your child struggle. I'm sure you don't want to do it that way. I am writing this book because I don't want you and your child to experience that much pain. I believe you are reading this book for the same reason.

Learning from your mistakes is much more difficult than it sounds. Painful experiences tell you what doesn't work but don't reveal what does. It can take years of painful and damaging experimentation before arriving at the *right* approach. At that point you

---

When it comes to helping your child, *working hard* without *working right* will generally do more damage than good.

---

have solved one problem but have created another—how to reverse all the damage those mistakes have caused.

Modeling Success

Experts, who teach how to achieve what you want in life, teach a better, shorter, and less painful way to learn. Nuero-Linguistic Programming (NLP), which is labeled the science of achievement, is taught by success gurus like Tony Robbins and employed by many top psychotherapists. Its most basic principle is *modeling success*. They teach that the shortest path to success is to study and learn from people who have succeeded at doing whatever it is you are trying to do and then following their patterns of thought and behavior.

When my son wanted to high jump in ninth grade, he didn't just go out and start jumping. We went online and watched a dozen videos of champion high jumpers. We watched the videos together over and over. We studied their approach, footwork, takeoff, and how they curled over the bar. We talked in detail about how they positioned their bodies before takeoff and what they did with their legs and arms once they were in the air.

Then he went to track practice and listened to coaches who had studied successful high jumpers even more than we had. They knew how those high jumpers trained between meets, how they warmed up before a vault, how they paced off their starting point, and what they focused their mind on just before they took off toward the bar.

My son learned to *work right* based on what successful high jumpers had done. Without that, he could have *worked hard* and *worked smart* but fallen far short of his potential. Instead, he qualified for the state track meet as a freshman.

Working right is simply much easier than *working hard,* much less frustrating than *working smart,* and the only effective way to accomplish a goal.

Getting Help

For my son, getting help from his coach was essential. Experts on what successful people do to succeed cite another common factor. They not only learn from successful people, they also get help from them. A friend of mine participates in a charity event each year that is sponsored by Michael Jordan. One year he had the chance to talk to him about the value of coaches. As great of a player as Jordan was, he gave much credit to his coaches' ability to point out things he should do both in practices and in games; valuable things that he couldn't see from his own perspective.

Getting help is hard for most of us—it is especially hard for those of us with ADD. Part of it is our history. In the past we have disappointed and frustrated people who have tried to help us. Our lack of follow-through makes us shiver at the mere thought of accountability. We may also feel that coordinating with someone else complicates matters. It seems simpler to our ADD mind to just put our heads down, isolate ourselves, and get a task done without the distraction of input from someone else.

An even more potent reason for not asking for help looms over our ADD heads. We feel that asking for help confirms all the negative opinions we perceived from those we interacted with growing up. We think that the only way to show that they were wrong is to do it on our own. Part of us says that requiring someone's help in order to succeed proves nothing.

Whether or not you have ADD, you may feel the need to shore up your feelings of self-worth by doing things on your own. We have all dealt with a child who at some stage in their development insists on proving that they can do it "by self." In fact, for some children it seems that from the day they learn the word *self,* they insist on using it every time they face learning a new skill. It is interesting to watch such children learn to tie their shoelaces or write their name. After much failure and frustration they eventually turn to us for coaching. Some of us stay in that stage of development for decades, insisting on doing things on our own, using only our own wisdom and skills. Unfortunately, stubborn independence is a pattern of thinking that goes against the way successful people achieve success. Getting help will make the path you and your child are on shorter, smoother and less steep.

Once again, I may be preaching to the choir. The fact that you have invested in your child's future by reading this book, means that you have realized the need to learn from others the best way to help your child through their ADD challenges.

WHO CAN HELP

If you understand *working right* you realize that it is critical to get help from the right person, not just anybody. You can get help for your child's ADD from many sources; however, NLP (Nuero-Linguistic Programming) and common sense will tell you to look for two important types of people. First, find people who have personally experienced the same challenges you are facing and have overcome them. Second, find specialists who have successfully helped others meet the same challenges you are facing. Ideally, the people you find to help you will be both types in one. If not, find at least one of each.

Health Care Professionals

At the age of thirty I decided I needed help. I started seeing psychiatrists, psychologists, and counselors, but with little change. The help I really needed was nowhere on their radar screens. Not only did they not recognize my ADD but they also did little to address my ailing self-esteem. It is surprising how few mental health care professionals have been properly trained in the diagnosis and treatment of ADD.

I have determined that many people in the mental health profession are a bit like the blind men who examined the elephant in the nineteenth century poem by John Godfrey Saxe. The first man felt his side and declared, "The elephant is very like a wall." The next man felt his tusk and with conviction stated, "An elephant is very like a spear." The man who felt his trunk declared him to be like a snake. The one who felt his leg was sure he was like a tree. The one who felt his ear just knew he was like a fan. And the one who felt his tail was convinced he was like a rope.

I am extremely grateful for the great discoveries psychologists and psychiatrists have made, especially in the area of ADD, but when it comes to dealing with an individual patient, they seem to diagnose them with the ailments they are most familiar with. Some even try to fix every problem with the same tools. My father-in-law could fix almost anything with duct tape and bailing wire. When I opened the hood to his 1971 Pontiac, I saw plenty of both. However, that narrow approach rarely works on the human brain. ADD can appear to the untrained professional as depression, anxiety, or a behavioral disorder. Genuine depression or anxiety can also appear to them as ADD. Various other coexisting conditions or disorders can also confuse the diagnosis and complicate the treatment. Without the proper diagnosis and treatment plan your child can struggle for years with little relief from their day-to-day difficulties.

In their defense, mental health care providers seem hobbled by the policies of insurance companies. In order to succeed financially, they must offer those services insurance companies will reimburse them for. I don't blame them for that. They are also stifled by the prevalence of lawsuits, being forced to follow a safe but less effective path through patient care. The usual result is that they make a diagnosis, prescribe medication, and offer a limited number of counseling sessions. Rarely can that offering address the steps you will learn in this book.

Legislators and Educators

Some people also have the false impression that legislators and educators are going to help solve their child's problems. I respect those caring educators who have educated themselves about your child's ADD. I know that the right teacher in the classroom can provide a much more effective learning environment for them. Seek out these caring individuals.

Legislators are trying to help by forcing more teachers to accommodate the special needs of certain types of learners. Their efforts help, but there is only so much they can do—and for only so long. Sooner or later your son or daughter has to go out into the real world. They will work for bosses and clients that don't understand and are unwilling to accommodate their needs. They will study and work in environments that are beyond the reach of an Individualized Education Plan (IEP). At that point how well you have followed the steps outlined here and advice from other people who have succeeded will determine your child's success or failure.

Possible Team Players

The following is a list of people you can recruit to help you in raising your child along with a brief description of what their role might be. Once again, make sure that each person you enlist, no matter what their title, has either personal experience with ADD or has at least been effective in helping others with the condition. Interview them and ask for their resume and follow up with their references. Make sure you and your child will be comfortable working with that person.

- *Teachers* can give you and other team members accurate assessments of how your child performs in all areas of academics and how they interact with adults and peers in structured and open environments, in groups, and one-on-one. Teachers may be the best source of feedback on the effectiveness of changes or treatments targeting your child's ADD.

- *Guidance Counselors* can outline steps you can take to get the most out of your child's education. They can refer you to other parents experiencing the same challenges and other professionals experienced in helping families deal with ADD.

- *Academic Tutors* can help your child with study habits and competency in one or more academic areas.

- *Social Skills Trainers* can help your child develop skills in age-appropriate interaction with peers. They focus on practicing social awareness, sharing, taking turns and negotiating wants.

- *Educational Advocates* can help parents and students navigate through the various services available in the world of special education.

- *ADD Support Groups* can help you understand ADD and exchange ideas and encouragement. Children and Adults with ADD (CHADD) has chapters organized in many cities across the US. These offer both educational meetings and support groups attended by people who can offer their support and who also need your support. Similar organizations exist in other countries and regions around the globe. For a more complete list of organizations go to www.ADD ParentingSupport.com.

- *ADD Coaches* can use their in-depth understanding of ADD to help your child overcome challenges and develop life skills to achieve success. They can work with you to develop parenting skills better suited for a child with ADD. They can also work with both you and your child to progress as a team on specific issues. Many ADD coaches work directly with high school and college-age kids as their ADD success partner.

- *Social Workers* can help identify family and environmental factors contributing to ADD challenges.

- *Family Therapists* can help you improve relationships and family dynamics and eliminate obstacles in the home to better support you and your child's success.

- *Psychologists or Therapists* can help your child overcome emotional issues aggravating their ADD symptoms, or they can help you overcome emotional issues blocking you from being a more effective parent.

- *Neuro-psychologists* can conduct neurological tests and interviews to diagnose ADD and other coexisting conditions. They can recommend effective treatment options and refer you to other qualified specialists.

- *Psychiatrists* can provide a diagnosis and prescribe and follow up with medication to help with ADD symptoms.

- *Pediatricians* can identify any physical issues contributing to ADD and give you general advice on where to go for help. They can also write prescriptions for ADD medication and monitor for any physical side effects.

Emotional Parenting

There are thousands of books on the subject of parenting and none of them can agree. I attended a conference once where the keynote speaker, probably unwittingly, contradicted one of the basic parenting tenets of the organization that was paying her to speak. The organization teaches the use of reward systems for behavior modification; she preached an ethics-based approach. Obviously, what constitutes good parenting is debatable and can be confusing.

I want to point out a few parenting pitfalls that tend to get in the way of you accomplishing the important steps in this book. If you are doing some of these things, it doesn't make you a bad parent. It doesn't mean you don't care or aren't doing your best. At least I hope not, because my children have endured some of these—I just didn't know.

Bad parenting comes naturally—or put another way, following our natural emotions will result in bad parenting. Our nature includes motives like pride, fear and . . . Okay, pride and fear are enough, and on those two aspects of our nature hang most of the emotional mistakes we make as parents.

PRIDE

Both good and bad pride exist. Good pride is the feeling of satisfaction we get when we work hard and accomplish something. It is something we feel internally, independent of those around us, independent of a need to impress, compare, or compete. That feeling of personal accomplishment and growth is a positive motivation to continue to strive and grow. That type of pride should be relished. It will only make us better parents.

The pride to avoid in parenting is outward pride, which is based on what other people do and think. If you signed up for parenting to look good to other people, you know by now the naivety in that. Maybe you signed up to not disappoint someone like your mother-in-law or a spouse. Or, perhaps you thought you would feel more accepted or connected to your peers from high school or college, or the congregation at church.

Maybe you started a family for all the right reasons but now that you have a child, you hope they will impress those same people or even a new group, like the parents at the grade school or at the soccer field. If this is the case, you have learned by now that kids tend to do things that step outside the perfect picture you have been trying to project. If they have ADD, they tend to do those things regularly.

If you are prone to embarrassment on account of your child, I have a book you should read. It's written by the Terrasi sisters, Gina and Patricia. One of them has a child with bipolar disorder and the other a child with Asperger's syndrome, a form of autism. The name of their book puts parenting in a better perspective. It's called *Shut*

> Pride and fear are behind most of the emotional mistakes
>
> we make as parents.

Up about Your Perfect Kid. They wrote the book because they got tired of hearing from the mom sitting next to them how many goals their son had scored, while their own kid was sitting in the middle of the field picking daisies. They wanted to help parents get over their pride (or embarrassment) and focus on what is best for their child.

Prideful parenting forces you to use quick fixes that can have negative repercussions. An example I read years ago in Stephen R. Covey's book *Spiritual Roots of Human Relations* has always stuck in my mind. His three-year-old daughter had opened presents at her birthday party and was refusing to share them. Since he was a college teacher in the field of human relations, he felt special scrutiny and expectations from the onlooking parents to resolve the issue. After a simple please did not persuade his daughter to share her new toys, he resorted to reasoning, bribery and then fear. After each method failed his embarrassment increased. Finally he resorted to force by merely taking some toys away from her and distributing them to the other kids.

He regretted that the quick fix, which ended his embarrassment, had sent his daughter the message that he valued the opinions of those parents more than the growth and development of his child and their relationship.

The bottom line is, throw away your vain pride. The proud feeling you are after is the one you will feel ten, twenty, or thirty years from now when your son or daughter sends you a Mother's or Father's day card with a note saying, "Thank you for always being there and always believing in me." Wow, will the pride swell then. Let it swell; you deserve it. If you worry about your pride now, that card may never come.

FEAR

Fear is actually the lesser of the two sins because it is a case of loving and caring too much. Your fear is for your own pain but only because you know how bad you hurt when they hurt. You have been through it before. You recognize the course they are taking and where it led to last time. Maybe it was a course you took in your own youth that caused you a lot of heartache. Maybe it was the course of a family member who always struggled in life and whose genetic traits seem to have shown up in your child. You just don't want your child to go through what they have. I know those fears. They have been my parenting Achilles' heel.

ANGER

The topic of anger is still about fear. The natural way to react to fear is with anger. Studies have shown that children take responsibility for their parents' emotional state. If you are depressed, they feel it is their fault. If you are stressed, worried, or preoccupied, they feel it is somehow connected to them. If you are often angry, they relate it not only to the behavior that triggers your anger, but also to their essential badness. If exposed to parental anger enough times, they will develop a general sense of personal badness.

Sometimes we can react to fear in ways that surprise us and that we later regret. When I was about ten, I sat up late with my brothers and sisters and watched the horror movie, *Fall of the House of Usher* based on the poem by Edger Allen Poe. Afterward, I lay in bed in the dark petrified for what seemed like half the night. Then a terrible thing happened. I had to go the bathroom. To get to the restroom I had to pass through the den, the kitchen, and the dining room, all of which were full of shadows hiding menacing evils. My imagination was in high gear. After the dining room was the entryway containing the front door, which any evil person could burst through. Then I had to continue down the hallway and into the bathroom, and walk past the wide bathroom mirror. I didn't dare look in the mirror. I might have seen demons who had joined me as I crept through the house. I was sure they would appear in the mirror as ominous shadows breathing down my neck. I finally reached my objective and shakily took care of business.

When I opened the door to leave, a dark shape stood in the doorway staring at me. My fear burst out in violent anger and I decked the demon with the massive power my adrenaline provided. I then sprinted back through the house, dove onto my bed, and buried myself under the covers. It only took a couple of seconds to reason that the demon I had decked was my older brother. I turned on the lights one by one as I went back through the house to see how he was. He was sitting in the hallway rubbing his jaw, just as shaken up as I was. He thought I was the monster.

A quote I came across recently reads, "He that fights with monsters might take care lest he thereby become a monster" (Frederich Nietsche, *Beyond Good and Evil, Aphorism 146*). As in my childhood example, fear can build over time as you go through each day with the dread of the next bad news from school or the next unpleasant attempt to get your child to comply with your constructive guidance. Other frustrations in life concerning jobs, finances, relationships, and health can combine to create even more pressure. Then, as in my example, you may be faced with behavior from your child that releases a monster you didn't even know was lurking behind your forced calm exterior.

Sometimes you won't be able to avoid feeling the fear, but as parents we have to recognize it and deal with it before we are to the point of unleashing the monster. For the most part I have been in control of my parenting fears. The times I have not, both I and my children regretfully remember. If you often find yourself reacting with anger to your child's behavior, and after repeated promises to yourself and them you are unable to control it, that is the definition of an anger management problem. Please get professional help. Many health care professionals specialize in helping people manage their anger. Many groups exist to support you in that effort.

RAGE

Extreme anger is often our natural defense against the things that frighten us the most. When someone in traffic nearly runs us off the road, it can sometimes throw us into a rage. Once we reach that level of anger we become like a runaway stagecoach—our actions and emotions are difficult to reign back in, even though the event that spooked us was two counties back.

Parent rage is a much more destructive force in this world than road rage. Exposing our children to this type of anger should be avoided at all costs. Even if it does not result in physical violence, it is a very real form of emotional abuse. Specialists in self-esteem have found that the younger your child is and the more intense your anger the more damaging and long-lasting effect it will have on their self-esteem. When they see rage, especially directed at them, they assume that something about them must be very bad to cause such intense distress. If that notion is reinforced by repeated episodes, those assumptions about their lack of self-worth will become cemented in their subconscious mind. It will take years of professional help to ever remove. For many it will remain at the core of their self-belief for the rest of their lives.

ABANDONMENT

Perhaps the most damaging face of fear and pride in parenting is abandonment. It is not a common mistake of people like you who buy books like this. I only mention it on behalf of some exceptions. Some parents' pride and fear is so strong that they detach themselves, either physically or emotionally. Their pride is covered—they aren't around to be embarrassed or have their personal standards violated. Their fear is covered—they are not there to anticipate or share in their child's pain.

Abandonment can come in various forms. A parent may sink more time and energy into their occupation where they feel more control. They may throw themselves into hobbies, sports, schooling, or even charitable volunteer work. All of these areas of life are important and even necessary for balance and self-actualization, but if they become excessive and draw you away from manning your parenting post, you may be using them as a retreat from an intimidating parenting battle. Take your needed breaks, but return renewed and ready to fight on behalf of your child.

To those who feel themselves withdrawing from their parenting battle, I simply say, hang in there. I have seen the intense regret of those who have abandoned their posts. To those who don't feel that the pain and struggle of parenting is worth it, or that they just aren't mentally or emotionally up to the task, I say, read on. Following the steps outlined in this book will change your parenting journey and give you the hope that you can see it through.

LECTURING

For the most part, I had enough control of myself and misplaced confidence in my ability to parent that I released my fear in a direction commonly taken by those who believe that enough knowledge fixes anything. While that notion is generally true, lecturing is not the best way to impart that knowledge to a child. If you ask my older kids about my mistakes as a parent, they will take only a moment's thought before telling you about my "four-hour lectures." And they would be only slightly exaggerating. My fear was that if they didn't completely understand the matter, they would continue to make the same mistakes and even bigger ones later in life. I wasn't okay with them feeling that pain, and the pain I would feel for letting them down.

If they had given me any indication that they understood what I was trying to teach them, I would have thanked them for listening and sent them on their way. The problem with that expectation is that I was usually telling them something they already knew or at least had heard before, maybe even dozens of times. The misbehavior

I was trying to talk them through usually wasn't caused by a lack of knowledge. In fact, my oldest daughter would say, "I know, Dad, but . . ." and then disagree just enough so that I felt I had to explain it a different way. She did know, but by not giving her credit for knowing, I backed her into a prideful corner where she was not willing to agree with me one hundred percent.

I continued to lecture right up until the age when they learned to more effectively use body language and facial expression to tell me they were not one bit interested in my expository essays. I could see the minute their eyes glazed over and they were no longer mentally at home. My wife and I finally asked them what we should do differently. Fortunately they were honest in saying, "Don't lecture. We can't take it. Yell at us, ground us, even spank us, anything but talk us to death."

It took me a while to break the habit. I am a teacher by nature. But, with the help of my wife giving me the cutoff sign behind their backs, I was gradually able to wean myself. Things went better after that, and my younger children benefited from my older children's honesty and our willingness to change.

INTERROGATION

A sidekick to lecturing is questioning, which I also fell into at times. I deflect the blame for this mistake onto my mother, but the reality is, since she did it, I should have known better. When she was bewildered by my behavior, her pet question was, "What were you thinking?" My response was usually a completely expressionless stupor of thought. She and I both knew that I had not been thinking at all at the time.

As a parent I appreciated the following Bill Cosby sketch. His son came home one day with a reverse mohawk and Bill asked, "What happened to your hair?" His son shrugged and mumbled, "I don't know." Bill then asked, "Was your head with you all day today?"

Be aware that, just like with my mother and Bill Cosby, you will rarely get a straight answer to direct questioning. They will feel like they are on the witness stand, being attacked by the prosecution. They may feel that anything they say will be used against them and silently invoke their fifth amendment rights.

By practicing the steps in this book, you will be building a relationship of trust between you and your child. Then, if you use non-judgmental and open-ended questions, your child may open up about their misfortunes. If Bill Cosby had asked, "What do you think about your new hairdo?" his son might have told him that a friend suckered him into it, that he was dreading going to school the next day, and that he was considering shaving the whole thing off. If you consistently respond without judgment, someday they will want to tell you what happened and how they feel about it.

OVERCONTROL

Another common face of fear and pride is control. You try to control them through micromanagement. You try carrots. You try rods. You are merely propagating a myth in your own mind. Control cannot be maintained long term. You might succeed for a time and usually only when you are present. Your child will learn to resist. They will learn to sneak and to lie. If that doesn't get you to back off, they will eventually resort to demonstrating their independence by intentionally doing the exact opposite of your expressed wishes. This may be self-destructive behavior, which they do just to prove their independence from your overcontrol. If they continue in that behavior they will eventually do it because of low self-esteem, a lack of self-worth, or perhaps even as an unconscious form of self-loathing.

The desire to over-control your child may come from pride. You may make them behave in public or succeed in school to spare yourself embarrassing episodes or to protect your image. It may not even be your public image you are protecting—it may be that you have always maintained a healthy inner pride of doing everything in life with a high standard of excellence. Since you have a diminishing amount of control over your child as they pass through adolescence, you will need to get used to the fact that they exist outside your bubble of excellence.

Fear can also drive you toward overcontrolling your child. You may try to eliminate any independence that will allow them to make mistakes. Out of love you want to spare them the discouragement and pain of natural consequences. Unfortunately, you will also spare them the opportunity to react and learn from their mistakes.

Although we are motivated in life by the desire to gain pleasure or avoid pain, not everyone feels these in the same balance. Some people, including most people with ADD, are more affected by negative motivation (avoidance of pain) than positive motivation. The fear of pain is more intense for most people than the desire for pleasure, and can often enliven the understimulated parts of the ADD brain.

I'm not talking here about letting them run out into a busy street to learn from getting hit by a car, or letting them smoke pot to learn how to avoid addiction. I'm also not talking about wadding up the rules and throwing them in the trash. Children with ADD have a love-hate relationship with rules and structure. The ADD part of their brain makes it difficult for them to comply with a long list of rules; however, they feel calmer and are more productive within the structure of clear boundaries and documented expectations. Your parenting instincts will tell you which mistakes will be too physically or emotionally damaging to allow. If you get fear and pride out

---

They feel calmer and are more productive within the structure of clear boundaries and documented expectations.

> Allotting them gradual degrees of self-governance
> is the key to helping your child develop self-control.

of the way and listen to those instincts, they will also tell you when to let your child learn on their own.

You can capitalize on those natural learning opportunities. You may notice that after a disappointing or embarrassing experience your child is more open to learn and explore new ways of doing things. While it is still fresh in their emotions, help them bring into their conscious mind how it felt, followed by a brainstorming session that will prepare them to do it differently next time. Then help them imagine how it will feel when they do it according to their new plan. As they get older they will insist on learning everything on their own, so help them get good at it while they are young. Allotting them gradual degrees of self-governance is the key to helping your child develop self-control.

Strengthening Your Parenting Intuition

Let me just briefly mention a very valuable but shifty parenting asset called intuition. In my experience a parent's intuition is almost always right. It is right often enough that if we always follow our intuition our children will be okay. It isn't actually parenting intuition that is shifty; it is the consistency in which parents can access their intuition that is unreliable. What gets in the way of our intuition is our shifting mood or state of mind, and our emotional priorities at a given moment. Emotions such as fear and pride certainly move our intuition from the driver's seat to the back seat. When I have taken pride and fear out of the way, and taken the time to calmly ask my intuition for advice, my children have been blessed.

Your parenting intuition will improve as you nourish it. I have felt mine expand every time I have exposed it to good books, speakers, coaches, and counselors. As you read and listen, some things

> A parent's intuition is almost always right. It is right often enough that if we always follow our intuition our children will be okay.

will ring true. Sometimes you will say, "Duh, why didn't I think of that?" This is your intuition recognizing the good stuff and absorbing it. You will still have to be calm and collected in order for your intuition to lead you through a situation, but it will be more prepared to do so.

PARENTING JOURNAL

Sometimes we need to be more intentional as parents—especially if our best efforts don't seem to be working. A parenting journal can help you see things more clearly and sort out what adjustments need to be made. At the end of each day, write in it what worked and what didn't work. Record what you did and said in your parenting role, and how your child responded. Express gratitude for any positive parenting you did that seemed to help your child learn and grow. Record your parenting mistakes and how they made you feel. Acknowledging negative feelings about yourself or your child may allow you to start the next day without those feelings. Most importantly, take a quiet moment to ask your parenting intuition for advice. Take notes on what it tells you to do about a situation. Record how you plan to react the next time you face a similar challenge.

To form a new habit we have to identify the new behavior we want to adopt and practice it consistently over a period of time. Use your parenting journal to identify and monitor the forming of new parenting habits. Once an intuitive parenting technique becomes automatic, you will be more likely to use it even when your intuition is not engaged.

AN EXERCISE IN PARENTING INTUITION

Here is a way to increase your trust in and reliance on your parenting intuition. The next time you are in the grocery store and see a frazzled parent overwhelmed by one or more rowdy kids, try to analyze where their parenting is coming from. Is it fear or pride, or both? They may be doing all the right things. If not, don't judge them as bad or good. They are doing their best, just like you have. Focus your energy on compassion toward what they are experiencing in that situation. That compassion will subconsciously reflect back onto you. They may be a single parent who barely made it through a stressful day at work. They may be simply exhausted from dealing with a child who never switches off. They may be dealing with any number of challenges with finances, health, or relationships. Who isn't?

Here is a way to make your best better. Picture what you would typically do under those same circumstances. Where is your parenting coming from? If pride or fear is driving your approach, start at the beginning of the scene and freeze it. Think of a time when you felt grateful for your child being in your life. Think of a good day when you really enjoyed being with them. Hopefully you don't have to go all the way back to when they took their first breath and the nurse laid them in your arms.

> Ultimately we are less judged by what our children did when they were growing up, than by how we handle it.

Once you have that picture, think what comfort, encouragement, and advice you would give that struggling parent. Picture them thanking you for your valuable insights and turning to their children and doing a better job.

Then, and this is essential, picture that parent's face in your mind and the satisfaction they are feeling from following your helpful advice, and then replace that face with yours. Make it you who had a better perspective and did a better job by following your great parenting intuition. To make it even more real, buy yourself a frozen yogurt for doing such a great job, even though it was just in your imagination. Then set that reward as your incentive for each time you get through a troubling situation by suppressing your emotional reaction and listening to your own great parenting intuition.

When I talk to people who are finished raising their children, I realize that ultimately we are less judged by what our children did when they were growing up, than by how we handle it. Let your pride then rest on your ability to connect to your parenting intuition in any situation your child presents. Let your fear be a positive force, driving you to react to any behavior in a way that will help them learn and grow.

Preparing Yourself to Help Your Child

Understanding Your Child's ADD

STEP 1

Coming to an understanding of ADD has an astounding impact on those who have it, or those who are caring for someone who does. You may be both of those people and you may have already experienced the positive effects of that epiphany. People say that finding out how ADD has impacted their lives is freeing. It frees them from guilt, shame, and even self-loathing. The title of a popular book on ADD *You Mean I'm Not Lazy, Stupid or Crazy?!* by Kate Kelly and Peggy Ramundo, depicts the typical reaction of someone experiencing the initial revelation about their ADD.

After years of struggle and failure without understanding why, your child may have accepted some logical conclusions about who they are, along with some derogatory labels. The logic behind those conclusions comes from parents, teachers, siblings, and peers. Most of them are not trying to be cruel. Some of them are even trying to help. Others are just calling it like they see it. A few, especially peers and siblings, may actually be trying to inflict some verbal bruising. Those few have their own challenges to overcome.

Deep down you know their logic is flawed. You know your child is not stupid because they are smart about certain things in certain situations. You know they aren't lazy because once engaged they

> Finding out how ADD has impacted their lives is freeing.
> It frees them from guilt, shame, and even self-loathing.

can work untiringly toward a goal. You know they aren't crazy because aside from their shame about underachieving, they are fairly content with who they are. However, without a better explanation your child eventually has no choice but to accept the ones handed to them by the world.

MY PATH TO LEARNING ABOUT ADD

My Initial Revelation

After years of sitting on sofas talking to psychologists and psychiatrists, I was better at coping with the stress caused by my struggles, but I wasn't any closer to understanding why I had failed in school and continued to struggle in the workplace. I was also no closer to making those struggles go away. The explanation came to me the way it has for many of my generation: through my child's diagnosis.

My son's third grade teacher talked to my wife one day about his impulsive, annoying, and sometimes aggressive behavior. She suggested we have him evaluated for ADD. I was curious. Some of the behavior she had described fit me as a child—my wife would add that it continued to fit me as an adult. I volunteered to accompany my son to his first visit with a psychiatrist. The doctor gave me a rundown on how ADD may affect his ability to focus, organize, and control his behavior. That meeting blessed me with an enormous "Aha!" moment.

When I suggested to my counselor at the time that I might have ADD, she pointed me to the book *Driven to Distraction* by Ed Hallowell and John Ratey. I read it, underlined it, and outlined it. It changed my life. I not only understood why I struggled at certain things, I also had strategies to overcome many of those struggles. I started making lists, setting alarms, and creating systems and environments that supported my success. I got a Palm PDA (personal digital assistant) and practically lived with it in my left hand. My life was much improved, but not yet right.

I Wasn't There Yet

Two problems still escaped my understanding. One was still ADD. Unbeknownst to me, I had barely scratched the surface of what I needed to know. I look back now and am amazed at what I still didn't understand about ADD and about how it was manifested in me. My diagnosis had been secondhand, through my son's psychiatrist. I was applying an incomplete and inaccurate template to myself and became discouraged when it didn't fit and my ADD would trip me up or hold me back.

I reacted to my incomplete success in my usual way—I went to the bookstore. I found other books on ADD. They helped. I saw that research on ADD was evolving. I hoped it had evolved enough. I learned about other disorders that often coexist with ADD. I studied them. I identified my anxiety disorder—what an important clue. I noticed that much of my early behavior looked like high functioning autism, so I studied that. Everything I learned improved my life, gave me hope, and drove me to find the next big clue.

Learning about Self-Esteem

I knew that at least one important piece was still missing. I finally realized that conquering my ADD was one thing, but overcoming the effects of growing up without understanding ADD was another. I had changed my conscious beliefs about myself, but my unconscious beliefs were deeply rooted and stubborn.

I dove into and digested books on self-esteem and Neuro-Linguistic Programming. I realized that without stripping out the irrational parts of my old thinking and replacing them with accurate ones, I could never feel whole or integrated. I would still react to situations in irrational ways. That information empowered me to change the way I viewed myself. I still occasionally get stuck on some old thinking from past perceptions, but now I don't get as discouraged about it. I know they can be upgraded to new positive perceptions.

CONSTANT LEARNING

My message here is simply that we can evolve through constant learning. Learning not only helps us improve, but it also helps us believe that life can continue to improve. Every time we learn something new, put it to use, and feel a positive change in how we act and react, it gives us hope. It tells us that our possibilities are unlimited. We become hungry to find one more piece of understanding that will unlock another piece of success.

With all I have learned about dealing with ADD, I know that information is currently available that I still don't know, and that even more will be discovered in the future. In fact, I am sure that the most important discoveries about ADD have not yet been made. If I stop learning now, I will miss them.

I always enjoyed fixing things around the house, until everything became solid-state and disposable. If I understood how something worked and all of its moving parts, I was less likely to break it during disassembly and more likely to get it back together so that it actually worked. Schematics benefited both me and whatever gadget or machine I was trying to fix. They allowed me to see the inner-

---

Learning not only helps us improve, but it also
helps us believe that life can continue to improve.

---

workings of a device before I loosened the first screw. The more you understand and can see inside your child's ADD brain, the more likely your efforts to help them will have a positive effect, and the less likely you will make matters worse.

The Treasure of Books

Throughout the ages books have been one of the greatest treasures of mankind. Without written language civilizations languish or decay in ignorance. Our civilization is not lacking in recorded wisdom; however, if we do not take advantage of the treasures we have, we will personally languish in ignorance as well. We will die of thirst sitting next to a fountain of water.

My oldest daughter stopped by my house one day with her children, who at the time were ages eight, five, and two. She found me sitting in my favorite reading chair digesting a book on the latest research and diagnostic methods for ADD. She asked me if I wanted to read another book she had read a few years earlier on raising children with ADD. I was comforted to see that she had turned to a book when faced with a challenge. I'm sure her children have already benefited from the knowledge she gained.

One of my favorite sayings is "Of all the things I knew, I did *some*. Of all the things I didn't know, I did *none*." Decide now to never stop learning about your child's ADD. It is one of the things I talk about in this book that your child will thank you for later.

Who Do You Learn From?

Now that you are convinced to keep learning, where should you go for information about ADD? Although we live in the information age, we do not live in the age of truth and clarity. A lot of good-hearted, intelligent people are trying to support you in your ADD parenting. Unfortunately they are often the ones not making the most noise. The ones usually making the most noise are those with something to sell or a dogma to promote. Some of these are honestly convinced that "the elephant is very like a rope."

As you go looking, you will find conflicting and confusing information, everything from special ADD diets and supplements to brain therapies and high-tech gadgets. Unless you want your child to be a guinea pig, stick with people who follow principles and methods that have been scientifically verified. Properly conducted scientific studies verify what works in the majority of cases, not just a few anecdotal instances. They form the safest path to helping your child with ADD. Having said that, I don't imply that you can never veer off that path; however, I do suggest you establish yourself on that path before exploring other less validated trails.

For a list of a few of the many books and other sources of quality information, visit my Web site at www.ADDParentingSupport.com. It is by no means comprehensive, but it is a safe place to start.

An ADD Primer

Here are some essential concepts about ADD. Please don't feel satisfied that this brief summary will suffice. The Computer 101 class at your local community college may help you understand what you see when you breach the back panel of your home computer, but it will not fully prepare you to swap out the motherboard or overclock your CPU. I include this section on ADD only to make sure you have the minimum understanding required to commence the steps in this book. Other learning from various sources will be needed along the way.

ADD STEREOTYPES

Let's start with the only information most people have about ADD, its stereotype. We use stereotypes to add personality to the definition of a word. They can never accurately apply to a specific person. If all someone knows about ADD is what is encapsulated in the stereotype, they picture a kid who can't sit still, constantly interrupts others, and leaves a trail of clutter as they scamper through a room. People with this limited vision expect kids with ADD to be disobedient, mischievous, emotional, klutzy, disorganized, forgetful, and impulsive. Do you see the problem with stereo-types? They tend to only hold the negative or abnormal qualities of their subject.

Having dealt with ADD for decades, in both myself and others, I tend to include other positive characteristics in my picture of a typi-cal ADD kid. I see them as creative, sensitive, enthusiastic, passion-ate, energetic, and loyal. I also picture them having some unique streak of genius that may be active or may still be lying dormant inside their head. I focus on those positive aspects when trying to help them get their ADD out of their way.

ADD SUBTYPES

As you learn about ADD, stereotypes will give way to subtypes, which researchers have defined to more accurately describe your child's ADD. The official subtypes listed in the DSM-IV (Diagnostics and Statistics Manual), published by the American Psychiatric Asso-ciation in 2001:

1. Inattentive type (AD)
2. Impulsive/hyperactive type (H)
3. Combined type (both impulsive/hyperactive and inattentive, ADH)

You will notice that throughout this book I consistently use the older term ADD instead of ADHD. When the H was added in 1989 it was thought that hyperactivity was at the root of all symptoms included in the disorder. This was an unfortunate assumption that not only propagates the false stereotype I previously described, but also makes it difficult for parents and teachers not versed in the DSM-IV to recognize and get help for those kids with inattentive type ADD—those kids who are quietly struggling and consistently failing without being an absolute handful. More recent technology and research has led some experts to believe that inattention is actually at the root of ADD symptoms, and that even hyperactivity and impulsiveness stem from a lack of attention.

Most researchers have expanded those subtypes beyond what is stated in the DSM-IV. They don't all agree on exactly what they are; however, considering their differing opinions is helpful in understanding that when it comes to ADD, one size does not fit all.

One particularly helpful way I have seen subtypes defined is using characters from the children's story, *Winnie the Pooh.*

1. *Winnie the Pooh* — Inattentive, distractible, disorganized. He's nice, but lives in a cloud.

2. *Tigger* — Inattentive, impulsive, hyperactive, restless, bouncy.

3. *Piglet* — Trouble shifting attention, excessive worry, easily startled.

4. *Eeyore* — Inattentive, with chronic low-grade depression.

5. *Rabbit* — Trouble shifting attention, inflexible, argumentative.

6. *The Honey Bees* — Irritable, aggressive, impulsive, defiant, disobedient, learning problems.

The last subtype, *The Honey Bees*, was originally called Troubled-type ADD. My coexisting OCD forced me to give it a proper name.

BRAIN CHEMISTRY

What causes all these subtypes in the first place? At its root, ADD is a neurochemical imbalance in certain areas of the brain. Nueroscientists have scanned hundreds of thousands of brains. They can determine by looking at the activity or lack of activity in certain

areas whether a person is suffering from depression, bipolar disorder, obsessive-compulsive disorder, anxiety disorder, dementia,
autism, substance abuse, head trauma, and yes, ADD.

Although not necessary as a tool for diagnosing ADD, brain
scanning technology has allowed neuroscientists to gather irrefut-
able evidence regarding the basis of the disorder. My own brain
scan several years ago clearly showed my ADD, along with evidence
of my OCD and SAD. Brain scans of people with ADD show two
telltell signs: inactivity in parts of the prefrontal cortex and in parts
of the temporal lobes.

Most recent research indicates that these two areas of the brain
along with several others are activated or stimulated by several
smaller structures in a core region of the brain called the limbic
system. This central coordination is required to accurately perform
tasks involved in completing and turning in assignments, interact-
ing with peers, controlling speech and behavior, and any other conscious task performed in daily life.

This coordination is done through electrical signals in the same
way the central processing unit in a computer communicates with
its various logic, storage, input and output devices. As these electrical signals pass through the brain they are handed from one neuron
to the next by the use of chemicals called neurotransmitters. Two
chemicals, dopamine and norepinephrine, have been found to be
most involved in coordinating those tasks which symptomatically
challenge people with ADD.

Whether you have or have not followed my overly detailed
description of the brain, understand this final conclusion. Simply
put, ADD is a problem in the availability and/or use of dopamine
and norepinephrine in stimulating and coordinating complex functions in the brain. Three of these functions, regulating attention
(inattentiveness), activity level (hyperactivity), and behavior (impulsivity), are at the heart of ADD.

EXECUTIVE FUNCTIONS

Neuroscientists have placed a group of these brain functions into a specific category labeled executive functions. Your child requires one or more of these functions to perform various tasks involved in managing schoolwork, such as getting homework started, staying on task, completing it in a reasonable amount of time, and getting it to school and turned in. They also require the brain's executive functions to be up and running in order to interact with teachers, parents, siblings, and peers in an age-appropriate manner.

Before advancements in the study of the brain we referred to these functions collectively as the *left brain*. The *right brain* was thought to contain the creative, intuitive, and passionate side of a person. The *left brain* was what kept the *right brain* from running away with itself. It was critical, logical and rational. It planned out how to implement our creative ideas in an effective way and respond to our intuition in a responsible manner. It kept our passions from leading us into misfortune.

Here is a fairly up-to-date list of the specific mental functions scientists categorize as *executive functions*:

- Getting and staying focused
- Staying alert in boring situations
- Starting an activity
- Transitioning between tasks
- Sustaining motivation
- Completing projects
- Organizing
- Prioritizing
- Making decisions
- Planning
- Managing time

- Remembering appointments
- Remembering lists or instructions
- Turning off at bedtime
- Turning on in the morning
- Establishing habits and routines
- Learning from past mistakes
- Anticipating outcomes
- Adapting to change
- Coping with chaos
- Managing frustration
- Regulating emotions
- Monitoring nonverbal feedback
- Inhibiting speech and action

If a person consistently fails at performing any of the tasks listed, neuroscientists say that they have some degree of executive dysfunction (EDF).

Specific dysfunctions can exist with or without the core characteristics of ADD, namely inattention, hyperactivity, and impulsivity. For instance, it is possible for someone to only struggle with the ability to prioritize and manage time. In that case they would not have ADD, they would have only EDF. However, most researchers consider it impossible to have ADD without being deficient in at least some areas of executive functioning. Inattention, hyperactivity, and impulsivity by their very nature will cause problems in focusing, planning, remembering, and inhibiting.

Forgive me for falling back on a sports analogy to illustrate this point. In order for a team to succeed it has to perform effectively in a variety of individual skills. For example, in basketball a team will succeed if the players are consistent shooters, accurate passers, physical rebounders, and quick defenders. If they are deficient in any of these areas they may struggle to win. If a particular spectator happens to be a neuropsychologist they may conclude that the team has certain areas of executive dysfunction (EDF).

On the other hand the team as a whole needs to be motivated, dedicated, coordinated, focused, and well-conditioned. These qualities usually come through the efforts of the coaching staff. If coaches are not effectively communicating and coordinating the efforts of the team in both practice sessions and games, these team qualities will be weak. As a result the players may struggle to rebound because of a lack of motivation, not a lack of physicality. They may defend poorly because of a lack of conditioning, not because they lack quickness. In this case a symptom like poor passing would be more prevalent throughout the team due to a lack of coordination. The source of these problems would lie in the central control system, the coaches. That same psychologically savvy fan may diagnose this team as having ADD with certain areas of EDF.

For the remainder of this book I will refer to all these symptoms as simply ADD.

WORKING MEMORY

Working memory is critical in almost every one of the executive functions. Just like a computer, the brain has various places it stores information; some are more permanent than others. Working memory is transient memory in that it temporarily holds only what is relevant for the current task. It will contain a mix of information we pull from our long-term memory with what is currently coming to us through our senses. That information has to remain in memory long enough for us to perform the task at hand.

In recent years my wife complains that while cooking she occasionally goes to the pantry to get some ingredient, but by the time she walks there, opens the door, and steps inside, she finds herself staring at the shelves wondering what she came for. This is a typical malfunction in working memory that is more common as we get older and our brain, just like the rest of our body, starts to atrophy.

In the ADD brain, working memory is either slow to develop or never fully develops at all. Information like social feedback, instructions from a teacher, or present objectives either never reach working memory or are not held there long enough to analyze them properly, process them fully, and act upon them effectively. Problems with working memory contribute to both the core symptoms of ADD and most areas of executive dysfunction. Following are a few examples of how problems with working memory can create havoc in your child's life.

Distractibility

For kids who are easily distracted the information in working memory is too easily displaced by new sensory input. The sound of the fire engine going by causes them to forget that they were in the middle of doing their homework. A comment someone else makes while their hand is frantically waving in the air causes them to forget the thought they were so anxious to contribute to the classroom discussion. An event that creates the slightest emotional reaction can instantly and completely erase from their mind any information related to their current objective.

Many potholes exist along the road between your child's math teacher giving out an assignment and them turning it in the next day. In my book *Pudd'nhead,* which is about my blessed but crazy early years, I included a section called "Forty Ways to Lose Your Homework." Many days, as my mother drove me home from school I would repeat to myself over and over, like a mantra in a Buddhist meditation, "Study your spelling, do your math. Study your spelling, do your math." But if anything happened that carried either positive or negative emotional weight, it interrupted my meditation. I would never think about my assignments again until the next day when the teacher began the spelling test or asked us to pass our math papers to the front of the row. Even if my mother asked me after dinner if I had any homework, I would honestly have no recollection of it. Fortunately, in most schools these days, the process has improved and working memory is subsidized by a homework calendar. Even with that prop, I would have had no recollection of having homework or a homework calendar, but my mother could have asked to see and maybe even been required to initial the calendar.

Decision Making

When a normally operating human brain goes to make a split-second decision, it loads as much relevant data into working memory as is readily available. It consciously or subconsciously recalls similar decisions in the past and the results of those decisions, good or bad. It then compares them to the current situation and analyzes any differences. It then extrapolates factors that may exist in the future. Finally, it arrives at a predicted outcome for each possible path of action. Only in cases of extreme emotion or irrational fear does the normal brain skip this process.

Your child's brain may bypass that process in most decisions they face. The result is failing to control impulsive behavior, repeating the same mistakes over and over, and not anticipating future consequences or their impact on themselves and others.

Productivity

A computer brain breaks down each job into minute instructions. It stores a list of these instructions in working memory organized in the order they need to be executed. As it works it crosses off each task it completes and goes on to the next one. In her book *The Disorganized Mind* Nancy Ratey refers to this process as *chunking*. She emphasizes that breaking an activity into small chunks and tracking progress is essential for people with ADD to be able to initiate effort, sustain momentum, and reach a goal. She also concedes that it is one of the hardest things for some ADD brains to do. From inside the mind of someone with this challenge, the process may sound like this.

"Wow, I'm really excited about the science project the teacher assigned. I can just picture myself at the science fair standing in front of my awesome display with the first place blue ribbon hanging from the corner and surrounded by a throng of interested people asking me how I came up with such an inventive idea. Well, I better quit daydreaming and get started. I guess I should first . . . um . . . um . . . um . . . um . . . Hum, I wonder what Jake is doing this afternoon. I really wanted to try out his new video game."

Defeating a video game is usually more complex than your child's science project—the difference is, most video games are pre-chunked.

Transitions

A computer also has to allocate a large chunk of working memory to track what it is currently working on. It keeps track of where it places each piece of data it is not using for when it needs it again. When it has something more important to do, or it needs to split time between two projects, it simply stores all the information on the current project into a special place in working memory, loads data for the new task, and goes to work. When it has time, it reloads the previous project and picks up exactly where it left off.

Ineffective working memory in the ADD brain can make transitions traumatic. Once your child finally gets organized and moving on one task, switching to something else means they will have to go through that process all over again. For those with ADD, the old saying, "Out of sight, out of mind," can be very real. The second your child looks away from something it may be completely gone from their mind.

Time Management

The computer brain also uses working memory to monitor how much time it has been working on a given task. Every event that happens in the computer is timed to the nanosecond. It uses these timings to coordinate the millions of tasks it may need to perform in a single given second.

If your child is doing their math homework and you ask them out of the blue how long they have been working on it, they may honestly have no idea. Personally, if I am interrupted from an activity, such as writing, I won't be able to tell you whether I've been working on it fifteen minutes or fifty. I marvel at the ability of an experienced point guard in basketball to instinctively know when the twenty-four second shot clock is about to expire. Their awareness of the passage of time is acute.

My poor mother always wondered why I never got home on time when I went to play down the street. If she had understood my time-tracking disability, she would have bought me a watch with an alarm and set it every time I left the house. She did realize that my brain would recognize something visual like nightfall. So, if she said, "Be home before dark," I was less likely to disappoint her. However, if I was playing inside someone's house, I could easily miss that visual cue. Those instances caused my mother much consternation. Whenever I was missing after dark, she always assumed I had been hit by a car and was lying face down in a ditch somewhere. Before too long she would send a search party out to find my mangled remains. It was traumatic for the entire family. I really did try not to put us through that, but some nights my awareness of anything was shorted out by an engaging activity.

If your child is not aware of the passage of time they also may not be able to estimate how much time it will take to solve ten math problems or review ten vocabulary words for tomorrow's test. The last time they performed those tasks their subconscious mind did not keep track. If they tell you it's going to take fifteen minutes, it may be a total guess. You can use egg timers, wristwatch alarms, cell phone apps, or computer programs to increase your child's awareness of time. Other devices can help your child develop a better awareness of the passage of time. The metronome has been used for centuries to help music students develop a sense of timing and pace. Other devices have recently emerged that specifically help people develop a better awareness of the passage of time.

A WORD ABOUT STRATEGIES

Many people with working memory problems have to externalize much of the information normally processed in working memory in the form of notes, recording devices, triggers, and anchors. For example, if I have a comment to make in class, I jot a word or phrase on my notepad to be sure that thought is still available when the instructor gives me the nod. My notepad is an extension of my working memory.

When your child's executive functions are not functioning, understanding what their brain is not doing well will enable you to help them create effective strategies to compensate. Just like the strategy my mother came up with for getting me home on time, hundreds of simple strategies have been devised for developing or externalizing each executive function your child struggles with. The steps in this book will prepare you and your child to work as partners in implementing the right strategies in the right way to overcome those ADD challenges.

> When your child's executive functions are not functioning, understanding what their brain is not doing well will enable you to help them create effective strategies to compensate.

A WORD ABOUT TEMPERAMENT

In recent years psychologists have focused increasingly on the role of temperament in learning and development. They have linked various temperaments to the likelihood, severity, and duration of a child's ADD symptoms.

Temperament refers to certain mental or emotional traits which are evident from the earliest stages of infancy such as shyness or sociability. They are considered to be a child's basic nature. Anytime you say that your child is naturally curious or naturally sensitive you are probably talking about something you have observed since the day they took their first breath. Some babies come out crying and others come out smiling.

One of my sons came out in constant motion. Although he was a fairly content child it was exhausting to hold him. He would rotate in our arms like a rotisserie chicken. The teenage girls at church loved him because of his smiling blue eyes and his striking white hair, but after about fifteen minutes of holding him their arms would be exhausted and they would be looking to pass him off to someone else. When he started to crawl he never stopped. He learned to walk and run on the same day. When he was two my wife and I made an Energizer Battery costume for him to wear trick-or-treating. It seemed to capture his basic nature; or should I say temperament?

You may have observed some of the following themes in your child's behavior over the years. They are considered to be in the realm of temperament:

- Active
- Adaptable
- Anxious
- Calm
- Carefree

- Controlled
- Curious
- Easygoing
- Egocentric
- Exhibitionist
- Extraverted
- Fearful
- High principled
- Hopeful
- Hotheaded
- Introverted
- Negative
- Overly dramatic
- Persistent
- Playful
- Positive
- Quickly aroused
- Reasonable
- Sensitive
- Serious
- Sociable
- Suspicious
- Thoughtful
- Unhappy
- Worried

A WORD OR TWO ABOUT MEDICATION

Whether or not to treat your child's ADD with medication is one of the two most debated issues pertaining to the treatment of ADD.

I will cover the second one in a later chapter. As the parent of a child with ADD, you are asked to make some tough choices. Don't be swayed by either side of the debate or by any social stigma attached to the issue. Only consider sound medical advice based on solid research, combined with what you feel is best for your child.

As this section has pointed out, ADD is a physical condition and, as with the treatment of other physical problems, a hybrid solution may be most effective.

If a stressed out, middle-aged, overweight, under-exercised and french fry–loving man goes to his doctor for a checkup, and the nurse gets a blood pressure reading of 150/110, a good doctor will suggest a hybrid approach to treating that man's high blood pressure. One part will be to discuss with him behavioral changes, explaining that he needs to go to the gym, reduce fat and sodium intake, and learn to manage stress. The second part will be to write a prescription for medication that has been proven in multiple studies to lower blood pressure. The doctor will know that focusing on behavioral changes without treating him with medicine to immediately reduce his blood pressure may result in his patient having a stroke during his first stroll on a treadmill.

Blood pressure medicine, like ADD medication, has a long documented and scientifically verified history of effectively doing its job while causing few side effects. Therefore, doctors do not hesitate to prescribe it to support a patient's battle against hypertension. Mental health care providers adequately trained in the treatment of ADD will want to take a similar approach with your child. They will feel that medication will be of immediate help and give the longer term efforts of changing behavior and developing skills a better chance of success.

Men will respond to their challenge of high blood pressure in a variety of ways. Some men will not work at changing their exercise and eating habits, and simply take medication for the rest of their life. They will survive but not thrive. They will continue to be stressed out, overweight, and out of shape.

Other men will try to change their behavior on their own. A rare few who already understand much about fitness and nutrition will succeed. The rest will continue to try and continue to fail by not working right, and may eventually give up. Their future is not much different from those who didn't try at all.

Another group of men will study the current approaches to exercise and nutrition, and enlist the help of family, friends, an exercise coach, and a dietitian. They will continue to visit their doctor regularly for checkups. They may even visit a counselor to find ways to reduce their stress level and change their relationship with food.

The chart below is my personal take on the various options for people dealing with high blood pressure. I am impressed with how closely it parallels the options for people dealing with ADD.

If a patient makes all the necessary changes to control his hypertension, at some point his doctor may say that he no longer needs medication. If genetic and environmental factors put him at high

Behavior	Medication	Result
No change	Ignore meds	Continue to feel bad, possibly die young
No change	Use meds	Survive longer, feel bad longer, take meds forever
Change habits	Ignore meds	Feel better, possibly die due to other risks factors
Change habits	Use meds	Enjoy a long healthy life, possibly discontinue meds

> Don't be swayed by either side of the debate or by any
> social stigma attached to the issue. Only consider sound
> medical advice based on solid research, combined
> with what you feel is best for your child.

risk for strokes or heart attacks, his doctor may recommend that he take a small pill every day for the rest of his life.

Be aware that the same is true of medication for ADD. Some may reach the point where they can be effective in all areas of their life without medication. Others, because of their current daily demands, may need to continue on medication until those demands subside. Still others, because of the severity of their ADD, may require medication for the rest of their life just to perform the basic tasks of managing finances, health, and relationships.

Your child taking prescribed ADD medication may make following the steps outlined in this book easier and more effective, and following these steps may allow you to reduce or even completely eliminate their dependence on medication. However, treating your child with ADD medication without taking these steps will not be nearly enough to help them fight through their ADD challenges and learn how to succeed.

Accepting Your Child

STEP 2

THINGS YOU DON'T HAVE TO ACCEPT

Don't Accept Limitations

Accepting your child's ADD usually comes as a result of learning and understanding, but not always in the right way. Acceptance for some means giving in and lowering expectations. Please don't do that. Accepting your child's deficits does not mean accepting limitations. ADD is not some omnipotent power that they are at the mercy of.

The most prominent organization for ADD information and support is CHADD (Children and Adults with ADD). One of their mantras is "Don't say, my child *is* ADD. Say, my child *has* ADD." They use those semantics to reinforce the fact that ADD does not define who a person is. What they accomplish in life determines who they are, and that is virtually unlimited, with or without ADD.

> Accepting your child's deficits does not mean accepting
> limitations. ADD is not some omnipotent power
> that they are at the mercy of.

For example, your child doesn't have to accept that they can't manage time; they simply have to accept that they must manage time differently than what is considered normal. They have to accept that they have to select a strategy, implement it, evaluate the result, and make adjustments until they develop habits that support whatever goal they are passionate about. I discuss this process in detail later in this book, along with the importance of passion and purpose. If you are tempted to skip to that section, resist. It is important that you undertake these steps in the correct sequence. Your mindset and relationship with your child is the foundation upon which your child will start to build their success.

I recently heard of a successful journalist with ADD who couldn't focus on one topic for more than just a few minutes. His solution? He bought several tape recorders and labeled each one with a different topic. He spoke into each one based on whichever topic was distracting him at the time.

Someone out there has devised a system or strategy for almost every specific ADD challenge currently holding your child back. If you have difficulty helping your child overcome challenges, don't give up; don't settle. Help them search for a solution that fits—it is out there.

Breaking through false limitations is a valuable skill and one that the majority of people on this planet never acquire. Once your child learns to manage their ADD they will be ahead of the pack.

Don't Accept Lower Standards

Here is a question I often get asked by parents of kids with ADD: "My child doesn't clean their room," or "My child is often rude when I ask them to do something," "Should I just accept that behavior because of their ADD?" My answer is an emphatic No! Allowing them to lower their standards has a direct impact on their self-esteem.

You will have to prioritize the issues you address and cleaning their room may not be on the top of the list. If it is, you are blessed.

You may also have to approach the problem in an unconventional way. However, you cannot give them the message that their ADD is an excuse for lowering their personal standards of being, among other things, trustworthy, loyal, helpful, friendly, courteous, kind, obedient, cheerful, thrifty, brave, clean and reverent. Yes, that is the Boy Scout law. As a former scoutmaster, it is one set of standards my children were encouraged to uphold, along with a clear set of guidelines for moral safety set out by the leaders of our church.

Some of the points of the Boy Scout law will be especially challenging to a child with ADD. It will take patience to get there, but never give them the impression that the standard is no longer important. The Cub Scout motto is "Do your best." Constantly teach your child that they will be happier and more successful when they *do their best* to meet these and other valuable standards.

I have not discussed scouting as an example of holding onto standards to convince you to sign your son or daughter up for Boy Scouts or Girl Scouts. However, just in case I did persuade you in that direction, allow me to give you an important piece of advice. Find a troop where the scout leaders understand and accept ADD. If you don't have a choice of troops, give the leaders this book or some other material to educate them on what they will be up against and how to help your child have a positive learning experience. Also, discuss with them your child's specific challenges and strategies to help them manage their behavior and complete badge work. Because of my own ADD I understood how my scouts with ADD thought and was able to keep them on task and out of trouble, even when other leaders had failed to do so. Again, I'm not trying to sell scouting, but if done right scouting can be a positive, kinesthetic activity for an ADD kid. Its structure of achievements and ranks is well chunked and can teach your child skills such as planning, preparation, leadership, and steady steps toward a distant goal. Okay, I am selling a little bit. I can't help it. Scouting, done right, is a great supplement to any other treatment for your child's ADD.

THINGS YOU DO HAVE TO ACCEPT

Time

You and your child will have to accept the fact that this process of overcoming challenges takes time. You will both have to develop patience and focus on progress, not perfection, without lowering expectations of the final outcome. You will have to accept that some less important issues will have to wait while you focus on one or two important ones.

> Overcoming challenges takes time. You will both have to develop patience and focus on progress, not perfection . . .

Jack Canfield is the coauthor of the *Chicken Soup for the Soul* series. He has also been a teacher of self-esteem and achievement since before the first *Chicken Soup* book was published. In his less famous book, *Principles of Success,* he talks about patient persistence as "The Rule of Five." He tells how when he was impatient about his progress toward a goal he went to one of his mentors with his frustration. He was simply told, "If you would go every day to a very large tree and take five swings at it with a very sharp ax, eventually, no matter how large the tree, it would have to come down." We don't have to solve everything in a day—we just have to be patient and keep hacking away at our goals.

Mistakes

You will also have to accept that mistakes, sometimes a lot of them, will be made along the way. One week I hired my sixteen-year-old

---

By making it safe for your son or daughter to mess up,
you will be opening the door for them to try, learn, and grow.

---

son to replace several broken windows around the house. I showed him how to measure and cut the glass and then went upstairs to work, trusting him to operate on his own.

If you've ever tried it, you know that cutting glass can be a tricky task. He came upstairs a few minutes later to confess that he had cracked his first pane of glass trying to cut it. I went down and gave him some additional tips. He also broke the next one. I encouraged him to take his time and be thorough. After he broke the third one he was upset, but I saw that with a bit more practice he could do it. After breaking the fourth and final pane, he was in tears and wanting to quit.

I was tempted to let him but I still knew he could master the skill and that quitting would reinforce the notion that enough failures justify giving up. I told him not to worry about the cost of the glass. I knew it would be a small price for an important lesson. I handed him some money and he headed to the hardware store to buy more glass.

He succeeded on the very next attempt and went on to replace the rest of the windows without breaking another pane. He felt powerful that he had persevered. I felt grateful that this challenge had occurred on one of my good parenting days.

By making it safe for your son or daughter to mess up, you will be opening the door for them to try, learn, and grow. It will teach them to see their mistakes as part of the process of learning how to succeed.

Your Child Is Doing Their Best

When I talk with parents of children with ADD they are usually bewildered about the motives behind some of their child's behavior.

My own mother often expressed her bewilderment in her favorite question, "What were you thinking?"

There exists a myth that survives among some parents and teachers about what kids with ADD are thinking, and I'd like to dispel it right now. I hear it way too often and it should not be among your beliefs. This myth is, "They are using their ADD as an excuse." I can guarantee you that no kid with a decent amount of self-esteem wants to be frowned on by teachers and made fun of by peers for constantly screwing up and underachieving.

What I teach people who entertain this myth is a philosophy I learned from wise counselors and came to believe in my heart. That philosophy is this: "Every person in this world does their *best*. The fact that your child tells you they don't have any homework, when in fact they do, doesn't mean they aren't doing their *best*." Huh? Really? Yes! Really!

Let me explain. The only reason people aren't more conscientious or kind, more logical or lighthearted, is due to three factors: their genetic nature, their past experiences, and their present knowledge. The combination of these three elements makes up our beliefs about pleasure and pain. And as humans we always act according to those beliefs. If a child embraces the role of goofball or loser, their belief systems are in need of repair. The only way that child will change their behavior is by changing their beliefs.

If you consider the three elements that make up our beliefs, you'll notice that it is difficult or impossible to change our genetics. Although we can't change past experiences, using the right techniques we can

---

The only reason people aren't more conscientious or kind, more logical or lighthearted, is due to three factors: their genetic nature, their past experiences, and their present knowledge.

change how we remember them and feel about them. However, our present knowledge always has to change first. Fortunately, of the three elements, our present knowledge is the easiest to change. Yours is changing right now. You are also learning how to help your child change not only their present knowledge but also how they perceive themselves. As those ingredients change, their beliefs systems will change and their behavior and performance will have no choice but to change along with them. They will still simply be doing their best but their best will be better.

DON'T MAKE IT PERSONAL

Isn't it ironic that the traits we find the hardest to accept in our children are often the same ones we have struggled with ourselves? That has been true for me and for many others I have talked with and observed. Our reaction to those mirrored tendencies, although unhealthy, is usually motivated by love. Those traits or behaviors may have caused us frustration or disappointment. We love our children and don't want them to feel that same pain. It is a natural loving response.

Even our positive traits may have been a source of pain for us. We may feel guilt about not taking full advantage of those abilities when we had the chance. Again, out of love, we may put too much negative pressure on our child instead of using more effective positive motivation.

My experience coaching basketball serves as a microcosm of this pattern of behavior. I've watched some fathers be too hard on their sons and overly critical of their mistakes. When I see this I imagine that father had the talent and opportunity to excel at some sport and feels that he squandered it. He may be riding his son in proxy of his younger self. He may even now be struggling in his job with a lack of motivation or dedication. He doesn't want his son to develop those same habits.

If you are having particular trouble accepting one of your child's challenges, look inside yourself. The reason may be there.

Letting Go

I attended a meeting once where Steven R. Covey explained the concept of letting go. He got someone from the audience to arm wrestle him. They grasped fists and at the word "Go!" they both pushed with their might. Nothing happened. Their grasped hands remained in the middle, trapped by their opposing forces. Then he had them try again. At the word "Go!" he immediately gave in to the other man's force. The other man then immediately quit pushing against his hand. He then pushed back and the other man pushed back. Each time he felt the other man push he gave in and then pushed back. Before long their grasped hands were waving loosely back and forth. He called the result a win-win situation.

Sometimes our children are putting so much effort into resisting our control that they don't see that what we want is really what they want. Sometimes in order for them to see it, we have to let go for a while. When we do, they will give up their resisting and do what they know is right.

I once sat and talked with an eighteen-year-old young man who was torn about a decision. He was very clear about what his parents wanted him to do. They had been hounding him relentlessly to point his life in a certain way. I gave him one piece of advice: "Forget your parents on this one. If you do it because they want you to, it may not

---

Sometimes our children are putting so much effort into resisting our control that they don't see that what we want is really what they want. Sometimes in order for them to see it, we have to let go for a while.

---

turn out too well. If you don't do it because they want you to, you may be giving up something important. Tune them out and tune in to your own feelings and follow whatever your heart tells you." As soon as he removed himself from the force his parents were applying, he did exactly what they were trying so hard to persuade him to do.

Sometimes you have to tell your child to study it out in their own heart and make their own decision and that you will support them in whatever they decide. Letting go will let them make the decision without being distracted by resisting your control. It also shows them that you value their innate ability to sort through an issue and come to the right decision. Don't panic if they don't decide your way. If it is the wrong decision they will sooner or later figure that out. As they do, they will uncover the ability to find the right answers within themselves and at the same time become more open to your advice. Don't spoil all that positive growth by saying "I told you so" in even the subtlest of terms. Just be impressed with their intelligent and thoughtful decision, and be grateful that you gave them the room to grow.

HELP THEM ACHIEVE SELFHOOD

Years ago I stumbled upon the concept of selfhood. Your children are in the midst of childhood, growing toward adulthood. You are currently in the midst of motherhood or fatherhood. If you survive parenthood there is the likelihood that you will achieve sainthood. People can reach each of those points in their life without ever reaching selfhood.

Reaching selfhood requires that we first know who we are and then have the courage to be that person. Many people in this world are quite miserable, simply because they have reached adulthood without understanding their own essence. They allow other people or the world in general to influence who they think they are and what they strive to become.

It's Not What You Want

Whatever you think your child should be when they grow up, let it go. Help them discover that for themselves. Even if you think the most practical thing for them to become is a stockbroker, don't mention it.

You may want them to grow up to be something you think you should have become. You may have had days when you thought, "If I had only been an orthodontist, I could be golfing on Tuesday afternoons and fishing on Fridays. Wouldn't life be comfortable then?" The truth is, no one feels comfortable or whole in this life, unless they are following the path to selfhood.

Think for just a minute on what you really want for your child. Is it to get a college education? Why? Because that is what people in your family have always done? Is it because it is something you wish you had done? Is it because you associate wealth and recognition with being a college graduate? I'm not saying that getting a degree is a vain or useless thing. It is a great means to a lot of good ends. If your son or daughter realizes that one of those ends is where they are supposed to be in life, they will pursue it on their own with relentless effort. If they choose a different end, let go of your desires and support them in theirs.

It's Not What the World Suggests

The world also has its opinions about what your child should grow up to be. It doesn't name specific careers like real-estate investor, but society tells them that they should have a lot of money, or a lot of education, or a lot of power over other people, or a lot of leisure time in exotic places. Notice the words a lot in all those pursuits. The world doesn't care so much for the content of that abundance; it mostly cares about the quantity.

I especially caution parents that have achieved a lot of worldly recognition in the way of academic or financial success. Your son or daughter may be distracted by the standard you have set. Those things may have nothing to do with your son's or daughter's happiness. You know that. Make sure they know that.

Examples of Achieving Selfhood

I have had the blessing to observe an amazing man over the last few decades. He never had a lot of money but always enough to support his family and save for the future. Most people would not consider him rich, famous, powerful, important, or learned. At an early age he tried a few things and discovered a few he was good at and enjoyed doing. He developed himself in those areas and became respected and trusted by people he worked with. I have watched him and his wife over the years quietly respond to anyone they noticed was in need. They are in their seventies now and have enjoyed a full life and are loved and admired by many friends and a large posterity. That is my ideal vision of a successful, provident life.

Years ago I came to know a similar man who had discovered his great aptitude in business. He explained to me once that for him making money was like falling out of bed. He seemed to sense when to get into a certain business and when to get out. In spite of his wealth, he was not lavish in his spending. In fact, I didn't know he was financially wealthy until I was sitting in a meeting with him and a discussion came up about a single mom with two young kids who was struggling to make ends meet. She had found a job but needed a car to get her kids to daycare and herself back and forth to work. At some point in the conversation he quietly said, "I'll take care of it," as he looked down and scribbled a note in his planner. The other people in the meeting seemed to know what that meant and nothing more was said about it. Within a day or two a grateful young mom was driving a solid but conservative used car. If this man had painfully clawed his way to wealth, while ignoring his true nature, I doubt he would have been as tuned into the individual needs of

> Achieving selfhood allows a person to feel integrated,
> like all the pieces fit together. The side effects of that
> are far reaching and extend to worthwhile achievements,
> relationships, and contributions to others.

those around him. His most important success was not becoming wealthy; it was becoming his true self.

I take my last example from one of my favorite books *Tuesdays with Morrie* by Mitch Albom. It is a look inside of a man named Morrie Schwartz, who pursued selfhood into the world of academics. Mitch related his Tuesday conversations with Morrie, who had been his beloved sociology professor in college and who was dying of Lou Gehrig's disease, which was slowly robbing him of his voluntary muscle control. Each Tuesday Mitch found Morrie in worse physical condition but with the same positive, caring demeanor. He had solitary moments of sadness about his condition and his fate, and frustration about the increasing burden he was to others; however, for the most part he remained full of gratitude for the richness and enjoyment of his life. I was particularly influenced by his rejection of prevailing culture, telling Mitch that he needed to create his own culture, one that supported who he was. Morrie understood very well the concept of selfhood. Although his life had a painful end, the fulfillment and joy he experienced is something we all should covet.

Don't Lose Sight of Selfhood

Achieving selfhood allows a person to feel integrated, like all the pieces fit together. The side effects of that are far reaching and extend to worthwhile achievements, relationships, and contributions to others.

Sometimes as parents we lose sight of what we really want for our children. But when we are thinking straight and put aside our fear and pride, we simply want them to be healthy and happy. We want them to make choices that will provide them with a life that includes friends, family, and fulfillment.

Children are typically in a nonstop identity crisis, especially during the teenage years. Don't let that continue into adulthood. Through the steps in this book, you can help them discover who they really are. Give them the freedom and opportunity to become themselves.

Empathizing
with Your Child

STEP 3

FIRST-PERSON PERSPECTIVE

If you have ADD yourself the empathy step will be much easier. It seemed like a snap for me. It was natural for me to tell my son, "Hey, I have ADD, too. I know how you feel." In reality I didn't know exactly how ADD felt to him. I didn't know at the time that ADD has different subtypes, which even today continue to expand. I didn't realize that even those subtypes are manifested differently based on various other factors:

Temperament	My son and I were different.
Place in the family	He was a middle child, I was the caboose
Family environment	Again, a very different feel.
Community culture	Mesa, AZ, in the 90s vs. Ft. Worth, TX, in the 60s

I also learned about other disorders that may accompany ADD:

- Learning Disability (LD)
- Tourette's Syndrome (TS)
- Obsessive-Compulsive Disorder (OCD)
- Social Anxiety Disorder (SAD)
- Bipolar Disorder (BPD)
- Oppositional Defiant Disorder (ODD)
- Conduct Disorder (CD)
- Narcolepsy

The list is long and varied. Each one affects the severity and type of ADD symptoms. If you grew up with ADD, understanding, accepting, and empathizing with yourself will naturally extend to your child. However, keep an open mind to the unique way your child is experiencing it.

SECOND-PERSON PERSPECTIVE

If you don't have ADD, empathy may be a stretch. Somehow you have to step into your child's shoes. In NLP (Neuro-Linguistic Programming) this step is called taking on the *second-person perspective*. There is a good chance you are already an expert at it. When you watch a thriller on TV or in the theater or read a suspenseful novel, how do you react in the tense part when the vicious villain is chasing down the main character who is in a seemingly helpless situation? Do you tense up, clench your jaw, or squeeze the arm of your seat? When the scene is over and the main character makes it out safely, do you finally exhale along with them? Does your mood become one of relief and joy? Aren't you imagining how they must feel and in fact, personally experiencing a portion of the emotions they are feeling?

Of course you do. We all do. That is why the entertainment industry is booming. We almost all have the ability to see a given situation through the perspective of another person. We just don't do it much without a music soundtrack.

When you empathize with someone in a movie you don't always agree with their behavior. In fact, in your mind you may be saying, "Don't go in the basement, not the basement. Are you crazy? Oh, I can't believe they went down to the basement." But when the villain appears, we forget all that and simply feel their anxiety and fear.

Empathizing with your child is the same. You have to keep the judgment about their judgment to yourself. In a movie script the writers make the character go down to the basement. For your child, their beliefs about pleasure and pain write their unfortunate actions into the script.

LISTENING TO EMPATHIZE

So far I've discussed the inward process of empathizing. The outward part of it is called listening. Listening is the only proven way your child will know that you understand them and empathize with what they are experiencing and feeling. Without listening you will also never see enough of your child's movie to become emotionally captivated by a given scene.

Five Steps to Listening Right

Listening seems easy enough. You may ask your child, "How was your day?" every time they walk through the door. But if you don't include the following five elements in your listening, it may seem like a dangerous question to your child. It may also be a frustrating encounter for you, and you may eventually quit asking.

> They must feel that you understand and accept their feelings
> before anything you say will be seen as relevant.

Until you master these simple steps, useful communication *from them* will be shut down. They will only share with you a meaningless portion of their life. They will bury their problems and hide their emotions. Your communication *to them* will also be cut off. They must feel that you understand and accept their feelings before anything you say will be seen as relevant. You will be helpless in helping them without knowing what is going on in their life, their head, and their heart.

1. *Make Quality Time*

First, you will need to find or create time for their answer to "How was your day?" Make sure you allow enough time to do some quality listening. It can be when they get home from school or when you get home from work. Make it a point not to be busy, or try to be doing something you can do while being attentive. If you have trouble getting them to stop long enough to talk, invite them to help get dinner ready or fold some laundry. Asking them to go shoot hoops or kick a soccer ball may also do the trick. Taking them out for a late-night ice cream or an early-morning breakfast will almost always work. Make it their time to say whatever they want without any coercion or judgment from you.

Also make sure you are in the right frame of mind. If you are too frazzled when you first get home from work, don't ask them questions you are not emotionally prepared to deal with. Do whatever routine you do to unwind. If you go to your room to change clothes, sit for a few minutes and meditate.

You don't have to be a Buddhist priest or yoga master. Meditation can be as simple as sitting in a comfortable position with your eyes closed, breathing slowly and deeply, and clearing your mind one thought at a time of any concern that is not relevant to the current moment. Once you feel calm and relaxed, get in touch with your parent within by focusing on what you really love about

your child. In your mind, go through a list of their positive qualities. Picture the last positive experience you had together and how
good you both felt. Then repeat in your mind one or two of your
parenting mantras. These are simply your core beliefs about effective parenting. If you are someone who believes in God and that
He is still your child's ultimate loving Heavenly Parent, you can
do your meditation on your knees in a conversation with your
Divine Creator.

With some practice your clearing, centering, or spiritual preparation will take just a few minutes, but it will have an important and
lasting effect in your child's life.

2. *Use Open-Ended Questions*

If, when your child gets home from school, you ask them, "Did you
get your conduct card turned over today?" you will probably get a
yes-or-no answer. Whether their answer is true or not, it will be the
only piece of information you get. The question has two issues. First,
it focuses on a negative, which shuts them down instead of opening
them up. Second, it is a closed-ended question, which they can normally reply to with a single word, giving them a natural exit point to
the conversation. Closed-ended questions, simply put, are ones that
have a yes-or-no or one-word answer. They make it easy for your
child to tell you what they think will appease you, instead of the
information you need in order to help them.

On the other hand, open-ended questions invite more information and allow your child to pick the direction they want to go and
the order in which they reveal what is on their mind. Your child may
have things to say before they feel comfortable sharing the information you need. They may test your mood before delving into their
real issues. If you get them started and then practice listening right,
you will eventually get everything you need and more—maybe not
today, maybe not tomorrow, but eventually.

> Your child may have things to say before they feel
> comfortable sharing the information you need. They may
> test your mood before delving into their real issues.

Don't let your open-ended question be answered by a single word. When I was in school, my mother would occasionally ask me, "How is school going?" My pat answer was "Fine." *Fine* can mean a lot of things. From the movie the *Italian Job* we learn that it stands for Frustrated, Insecure, Nervous, and Emotional. That always fit me when it came to facing my mother about schoolwork. *Fine* can also stand for Feeling Inadequate and Needing Encouragement.

If your child ever tells you that something is *fine, okay,* or *all right,* know that it is code for "slowly sinking" or "failing miserably." Let it be your cue to invite them to share. Your response to "fine" can be as simple as, "Tell me more," or "How so?" Let them know that you really do care and are willing to take the time to listen and understand.

Here are a few excellent open-ended questions you can try with your child. Notice that none of them pry into either their behavior or their emotions. They simply get your child talking about their day.

- What did you do at recess today?
- What are you working on in art?
- What book are you reading during reading time?
- What are you studying in science?
- Who did you sit by at lunch today?

3. *Withhold Judgment*

Your child will clam up at any whiff of judgment. When you sense they are ready to open up to you about their day, that is when you have to remind yourself that whatever they did was their best, based on their genetic makeup, past experiences, and present knowledge. You may be tempted to jump in and upgrade their present knowledge right then and there. Resist! It's not the right time. At this point they will only see advice as judgment. For now just bite your tongue and listen to every word they say. If you *listen right*, you will know when to offer your sage counsel. Someday they may even shock you and ask for it.

When you first start practicing listening right your child will be hypervigilant to your reactions. They will monitor your body language and facial expressions with elevated senses. If you are like me, you have a hard time being emotionally opaque. Have you ever asked your child to do something you have asked them to do several times already and are now frustrated about their lack of follow-through? I have coached myself on body language and facial expressions before these types of encounters. It helps, but sometimes my attitude still leaks through.

If you are having problems maintaining a nonjudgmental aura, practice in front of a mirror or with your spouse or a friend. Have another person play the part of your child and relate some ridiculously ignorant mistake. Do the first role-play without speaking, where you exaggerate your worst, most judgmental and emotional body language and facial expressions. This will help you identify what not to do. The second time, do your best and have your partner rate how comfortable they would be continuing to share. If they are not completely comfortable, discuss specific nonverbal adjustments and try it again.

Once your child feels comfortable that you are listening without judgment, you can follow up with questions that help them reveal their own judgment about what they have shared:

- What was your favorite part?
- What was your least favorite part?

- What did you feel like doing?
- How did that make you feel?

4. Convey Understanding

Listening right ironically requires some talking. Your child has to have reassurance along the way. If you say nothing they will try to read your mind. They may assume you are not responding because you don't understand or because you are suppressing a negative response. You have to give them indications along the way that it is safe to continue.

Interject summary statements that demonstrate that you are present and listening, and that you understand the circumstances they are describing. Don't be obvious in parroting back to them everything they say like some overachieving therapist. They will get wise to you if every response begins with, "So, what I am hearing you say is . . ." followed by their exact words.

If you are truly engaged, you will be more artful about it without much effort at all. Point out facts that may be important to them, like, "Isn't Derrick the kid that picked on you last week?" or "You had three tests in one day?" Putting what they say into your own words or clarifying facts without turning it into an interrogation indicates that you understand and care.

Since you have to speak, it is important to use the right tone of voice. Sometimes that can be the most difficult part. You can mimic the right words to say but sometimes they seem to come out emotionally charged. Your child will pay more attention to your tone than your words.

Keeping your tone soft and calm is easier if you speak at a slower pace than you normally do. The slower pace not only adds calmness to your voice, but it calms you and puts you into a more receptive state. If you find yourself struggling with maintaining the right tone, you will need to practice. Practice in the mirror or role-

---

Your child will pay more attention to your tone
than your words.

---

play with your spouse, friend, or coach if you have one. You will master it quickly with just a little practice. Once you hear the right tone coming from you and the calm feeling that it invokes, you will start doing it quite naturally and your child will become more apt to share.

5. Validate Feelings

Once your child is feeling understood, your next step is to make them feel valid. Their actions or reactions to the experience they are sharing with you may not have been valid, but how they feel about it always is. Our feelings are at the core of who we are. If we conclude that our feelings are invalid, we are conceding that something is seriously wrong with us. We can change how we deal with our emotions and with practice we can even learn to change one feeling into another, but our original feelings are natural—they are what is human about us.

It doesn't matter at this point that their bad judgment created the bad experience. At some level of their consciousness they already know that. What is important is that both you and your child recognize and acknowledge how it felt. That is where your empathy skills really get their workout. Your child may not even know or be able to express how they felt. You may have to put yourself into their exact circumstances in order to see for yourself.

Here is an exercise in putting on your child's shoes that you can adapt to their specific situation. The first few times you try this you may need a few minutes alone in a quiet place in order to slip them on, lace them up, and walk around a bit.

Picture yourself sitting in a classroom surrounded by kids who you think look down on you because of all the things that have happened over the course of the school year. Picture facing a teacher who you feel has been constantly disappointed in your efforts. Picture looking up at that person who is twice as tall as you and seems to hold your fate in their hands every second of the school day. Then imagine yourself sitting at your desk when you suddenly realize that once again you forgot to read the assigned chapter in your science textbook and answer the questions at the end. Just then the girl sitting across the aisle from you turns her back toward you to talk to another classmate. You see her homework paper on her desk ready to be passed to the front of the row.

Can you see how that level of empathy can help you react without judgment? At this stage in your life you could easily resist the temptation to copy her answers. But, if you truly put yourself in your child's physical surroundings and emotional state of mind, you can usually see why they did such an unfortunate thing. You don't have to approve of their actions; I doubt they do, either. You only have to recognize the fear of humiliation your child faced at the precise moment they decided to quickly copy their neighbor's answers, minutes before the teacher asked them to pass their homework to the front of the room. You also have to identify the anger they felt when the kid behind them ratted them out, the shame they felt from being publicly identified as a cheater and a slacker, and the fear and isolation of having to walk the long hallway to the principal's office. You have to know about the dread they carried around the rest of the day, knowing that you would be getting a phone call from their school, and that they would have to face your disappointment and discipline and possibly your condemnation and anger.

If they are not yet expressing the emotions they experienced, fill in what your best shot at empathy is telling you. The dialogue for this is as simple as that used to convey understanding. Short phrases like, "That must have made you sad," or "That must have made you angry," will work just fine.

Once you give their feelings a name, pause and let them respond in their own words how it felt. The pause is important. It tells them that your guesses about how they felt are only guesses and that their opinion on the topic of their inner feelings is the only one that matters.

DON'T GET OFF TRACK

The process outlined is simple: make quality time, use open-ended questions, withhold judgment, convey understanding, and validate feelings. Stick to these simple steps, and don't get off track. Here are a couple of ways we tend to get off track.

Men and Empathy

This topic is a special warning to us fathers. It is common knowledge that we are generally not as good at listening as mothers are. I have a daughter who will eat chicken, but she could never pick a chicken out of the henhouse, chop its head off, pluck it, skin it, and chop it into pieces. She empathizes too much with the poor chicken who was just minding her own business eating scattered chicken feed when the whole gruesome process commenced. If she is that tuned into a chicken she has never met, think how good she is at empathizing with the two adorable girls she cares for every day and kisses and tucks into bed every night.

For the most part we men have no problems preparing a chicken for a hearty meal. We are genetically programmed to have a harder time empathizing. Our thickheadedness helped us survive and defend our families during less civilized times. I'm not saying that we are incapable of empathy, that it is not within us. Some fathers are very good at it, just like some mothers are not. All of us need varying amounts of practice—I'm just saying that fathers tend to need more.

Fathers are also genetically programmed to fix things. That tendency can really get in the way of listening. I realized that for the first time when my oldest daughter was about twelve. She was upset about our recent move from Texas to Arizona and the challenge of making new friends. I invited her to open up to me. Less than two minutes into our conversation I was dispensing to her what I thought were fairly wise solutions. Instead of the gratitude I naively expected, she burst into tears. I realized right then and there that my nature was getting in the way of helping her. So, I gave her the wisest advice I could at the moment—I suggested she go talk to her mother. It turned out that all she needed was understanding and empathy. She had already worked out some great solutions on her own.

I learned this concept even more clearly from a talented and very empathetic school psychologist, Terry Illes, whom I met through CHADD. He taught, "Helping your child feel better about a problem may be more useful than trying to eliminate the problem." My wife instinctively knew that all my daughter needed was to feel better about her situation. She also sensed that the best way to help her feel better was through empathetic listening.

Focus on Their Emotions, not Yours

Invariably during these listening sessions, your child will say something you will have an emotional reaction to. For example, something they say may trigger your parental nature to defend your offspring. You may want to march right down there and . . . Suppress this impulse for the time being. Later you can get their permission to do any "giving what for" that is proportionate and appropriate.

Sometimes your child will push your buttons unintentionally. Something they relate may stir up emotions about a similar experience in your past that they have no knowledge of. Again, recognize and acknowledge those emotions to yourself and then let them go.

Allow this conversation to be their time to deal with their feelings, not yours.

Your child may at times intentionally push your emotional buttons. They are testing your commitment to your calm facade and nonjudgmental stance. While I was serving as cabin dad at my son's fifth grade science camp, one of the boys in our cabin became very emotional and angry for seemingly no reason. I invited him out onto the front porch to talk. I asked him to share with me what was bothering him. The first thing out of his mouth was, "I just really hate your son."

He subconsciously knew that if I reacted calmly to that button being pushed, he could trust me enough to share his real emotions. I suppressed my own emotional reaction and asked him with genuine interest why he hated my son. I listened as he spewed out some irrational reasons. I paraphrased what he related and stated from his perspective how it must have made him feel.

He never shared with me what was really bothering him. Our brief conversation didn't generate that much trust. I had observed him a couple of times with his own dad and saw the judgment and pressure he was under. Based on that, I made an empathetic guess that he was jealous of the open and supportive relationship my son had with me that week. I couldn't do anything about his relationship with his dad, but just listening to him vent allowed his frustrated and agitated mood to dissipate. He was then able to rejoin the group with a much more cooperative attitude, which he kept for the rest of the week.

THE RESULT OF LISTENING RIGHT

With a little practice and restraint you will become better at these steps and appropriate feelings of understanding and empathy will come more easily. If you are consistent over time, the results will become evident.

Most of the benefits will show up simply as a happier child. The number of traumatic experiences they come home and relate to you will decrease. When they do come home distressed, their emotions will be less intense. They will start to recognize their emotional responses and empathize with themselves before they get to you. When they do share with you, it will be a different conversation. They will tell you what happened to them that day without prompting and share how they felt about it. Then they will go out to play.

Another benefit that will appear is an improvement in your child's ability to pay attention. Unrecognized or unresolved emotions can be a major distraction for anyone. Since ADD is driven by an attention deficit, the less their emotions are distracting them the more they will be able to pay attention to other things in their life. By listening right you will help them lay their emotions out on the table and then fold them neatly and put them away, freeing them to pay more attention to the present.

Without such intense emotional distractions another change will appear. Your child will start to calmly and rationally come up with appropriate responses to situations and solutions to problems. Their own solutions will amaze you. Then, one day, the most amazing thing of all will happen. No one can say how long it will take, but if you are consistent long enough, the day will come when they will solicit your advice. Wow! That day will be the day they realize one of the most important things in life: we can't do it on our own.

People with ADD have a tendency to be independent and stubborn. It is hard, even painful for us to open up to help from others.

By listening right you will help them lay their emotions out on the table and then fold them neatly and put them away, freeing them to pay more attention to the present.

Ironically, input and even assistance from others is essential to our progress and success. As we are figuring out how to compensate for our brain deficiencies, we need to model what other people have done to succeed. We need unbiased feedback to make us more self-aware. We need caring people to provide points of accountability. When we get stuck we need a well-informed spouse or friend or even a skilled coach to help us shift gears.

In order for your child to form that partnership with you as their parent coach, they must trust you to be understanding and empathetic. That partnership is the goal. It is the platform for your parenting success. One essential pillar of that partnership is your ability to listen right. Strengthen that pillar through regular practice, self-assessment, and conscious adjustments.

Focusing on
Your Child

SECTION THREE

Your Goals in Helping Your Child

This section will help you help your child succeed at tackling the four toughest challenges of ADD. These four challenges are not: earning good grades, staying out of trouble, keeping a clean room, and making new friends. Those goals are important and often challenging but you need to look past them for now.

Goal 1   You need to help your son or daughter understand and accept the unique way their brain works and how it is impacting their life.

Goal 2   You need to zero in on what I call their superpowers: those things they do well, easily, and enjoyably.

Goal 3   Once you arm them with self-awareness, they need a healthy, whole self-esteem. They need to realize that in spite of their struggles they are worthy of a happy and fulfilling life.

Goal 4   You need to help them believe that no matter what challenges seem to obstruct their path, with courage and persistence they can achieve success. That belief will foster the motivation required to put effort into forward motions.

If you can accomplish those four goals, the two of you are ready to move forward in a big way. If you don't accomplish them, nothing else will matter. No successes you force out of them at school or in any other activity will allow them to avoid a life full of fear and frustration.

Help Them
Understand and
Accept Themselves

GOAL 1

So, let's get started with *Goal 1* which is to help your child understand and accept themselves.

FOCUSING THE BLAME

Once you personally start to understand and accept what your child is up against, and have gained their trust through empathetic listening, you are ready to help them understand and accept their challenges, and have that same empathy for themselves.

If they don't understand that brain chemistry is behind their struggles at school and in social situations, who and what will they blame? I'll tell you. Your son or daughter will take on all the blame and punish themselves for being lazy and stupid. They will try again and again not to be those things any more, but after each failure they will beat themselves up and hate themselves more. They will eventually find the courage to try again, with even more determination, but with more stress and more anxiety about the outcome. Without understanding what they are up against, your child will fail again, and when they do they will feel even more disappointment and self-loathing. They will be in a vicious downward cycle that has a bitter bottom.

TALKING ABOUT THEIR ADD

Talk about their ADD the same way you would any physical deficit. I have a young grandson who developed knocked knees at about the age of three. He is rather short for his age but he runs like the wind and is a blur on the soccer field. When he runs he reminds me of the boy named Dash in the movie *The Incredibles*. His parents don't talk about his knocked knees behind closed doors. He knows all about them and is not ashamed of them. They may even contribute to his superpower (his speed).

When my son was diagnosed with ADD, he was lucky that I was diagnosed at the same time. I was so excited to have ADD instead of just being crazy that we practically celebrated it. We didn't whisper about it and sit around asking, "Wow, what now?" The fact that his brain worked differently than other kids in his class was okay, now that we knew how it worked and could focus on solutions. When he won the city math championship in fifth grade, we gave his ADD part of the credit. Not having a normally functioning brain was just fine.

DIFFERENT IS NORMAL

If your car has an automatic transmission you just shift it into drive and push on the gas. If your car has a five-speed manual transmission you can't just sit in the driver's seat lamenting the fact that you are stuck with a defective car. You have to have someone show you how to use the clutch. They may need to ride along with you and coach you for a while. You will have to learn to watch and listen to your RPMs and shift at the appropriate time. With time you will be able shift smoothly. It will become what some psychologist call automatized, so that you don't have to think about it and can do it while changing lanes, carrying on a conversation, and adjusting the radio. You will then have a skill that a lot of other drivers don't have. High-performance race cars have manual transmissions; so do large powerful trucks. In certain situations a standard transmission is faster and more powerful, and you will be an expert at using it.

When your child starts to understand and accept their unique brain wiring, they can start to convert those features into assets instead of liabilities. What a powerful person they will see in themselves! They will start to believe that anything in life is possible. They will feel like the amputee that runs a marathon, the woman with a lisp who anchors the news, the five-foot-two kid who makes the basketball team, the woman with dyslexia who earns a master's degree from Harvard.

They will feel like thousands of other people with ADD who have focused on their strengths, compensated for their weaknesses, and fought and struggled and didn't quit, and went on to be exactly who they were meant to be and to do exactly what they were born to do.

That's right. It all starts with understanding and accepting the ADD part of who they are.

Help Them Find Their Superpowers

GOAL 2

This goal is both fun and easy. Your son or daughter will especially enjoy it. So, not long after your initial conversations about what their ADD is, start to help your son or daughter discover their "superpowers."

Each superhero from the first DC comic until now has had specific, unique powers. Consider the Fantastic Four, for instance. Mr. Fantastic was elastic; Human Torch could fly through the air as a streak of fire; Invisible Woman could become invisible and form impenetrable force fields; and Thing was made of indestructible rock and could throw a semitruck the length of a football field. The Incredibles were the same way. As Mr. and Ms. Incredible raised their kids they watched for their superpowers and helped them recognize and utilize their unique strengths.

Your child has strengths, many of them. You may already be able to list a few. You will discover many more as you watch for them over the years. Perhaps some of them have not yet matured. Become a detective; a talent scout. Analyze their successes at and away from school, no matter how trivial they may seem. What skills and talents did those successes require? Notice which activities or assignments they enjoy. They will normally enjoy the ones that come easily to them. Easy usually indicates a natural ability—a superpower. Notice the topics and activities that interest them and capture their attention for long periods of time. If they are content to do something for hours as a child, they may be content doing it for eight hours a day as an adult.

Put your child into a variety of situations and activities. Their superpowers may not be manifested until they meet a specific problem or challenge. Sometimes I see parents curtail their child's activities because of poor grades at school. They insist that they spend every evening hitting the books. What a shame. Your child needs to have a balance and variety of activities in order to develop in life and find out who they are and aren't. When my children were about the age of eight we signed them up for a year of piano lessons. At the end of the year they either discovered a talent, which they continued to develop, or they were content going through life with only a basic understanding of music.

Be sure to include their soft skills. They are easy to overlook or discount but they are the most important skills in life: the ability to show love, to empathize, to be imaginative when solving problems, to not give up when something is hard. Patience, enthusiasm, friendliness, helpfulness, and honesty are all more important skills than being able to remember to turn in their homework. Add any positive qualities you observe to your list. Let your child know how important these are. My wife once told me she would rather be married to a pudd'nhead than a jerk. So, my soft skills have earned me over thirty years of being happily married. What a great success.

Once you and your child have made an initial list of their superpowers, take them out for an inspiring movie and some popcorn to

---

Be sure to include their soft skills. They are easy to overlook.

celebrate what an amazing kid they are. How do you think they will feel on the way home from the movie? I'll tell you. They will be sky-high. If human flight wasn't on their list of superpowers, they will think it is. They will feel valuable, powerful, loveable, and ready to go to work.

Now put the list somewhere conspicuous. Add to it often. Review it often. Review it when your child has a bad day at school. Review it when you are having a rough parenting day and may be running short on patience and perspective. At times when they get down on themselves take them to use their superpowers. If they are good at skateboarding, take them to the skatepark. If they are good at building castles out of Legos, get down their bucket of Legos. If they are artistic, have them color or draw you a special picture. If they love to read, take them to the library. Then praise them and compliment their expertise.

Being reminded how good they are at some things will help them work at the things they struggle with. I have one granddaughter who at the age of seven could read like the wind. She was reading small books at the age of five and chapter books at the age of six. My other granddaughter who is a year older was lamenting to my wife one day that unlike her cousin, she reads slowly. My wife pointed out to her that she may be right but that she really understands and remembers what she reads. She simply replied, "You're right, grandma. I really do get a lot out of what I read." Then she contentedly padded off to bed. She was totally okay with not having the superpower of speedy reading if she knew she possessed the strength of mindful reading. Knowing that strength will motivate her to keep reading, and as she does her reading speed will gradually increase.

ATTACK IT WITH THEIR STRENGTHS

Armed with an ever-growing understanding of their ADD and an ever-growing list of their superpowers, your child is ready to attack their villains. When Human Torch faced a supervillain, he didn't try to squash him with a ten-ton truck like Thing. He flew through the air and rained atomic fireballs down on him. Some superheroes, like Superman, had many powers like flight, super strength, x-ray vision, and super hearing. Batman made do with agility, superior logic, and technology (fast vehicles and nifty gadgets). Regardless of how they were endowed, their solutions to difficult situations always came from their own individual strengths, and they all excelled. You and your child have to follow their examples.

Also, when the two of you pick a problem to solve, make sure they attack it with *their strengths,* not yours. Keep the long-term vision in mind. Someday you won't be there. If they have relied on your strengths to meet their challenges, they will be experts at recognizing your strengths and putting them to good use. They need to develop the ability to see and follow their own path to success.

If they can't remember to brush their teeth in the morning, don't remind them each day. That would be using your strength, not theirs. You also can't tell them that they have to come show you their clean teeth every morning. That would require them to remember two things: brushing their teeth and showing them to you.

What if one of their strengths is building stellar structures out of Legos? Each time they brush their teeth they could get a Lego block out of a box in your room and add it to their brilliantly conceived Lego structure. After a week of not missing, they can have the entire box of Legos to play with for the weekend. After four weeks of not missing you could take them shopping for the latest new set of Legos. Four weeks of Legos, four straight weeks of brushing their teeth—a habit is formed. How easy was that? Your child's own passion for using one of their superpowers jumped in and did all the work.

Protect and Repair Their Self-Esteem

GOAL 3

I mentioned earlier what a significant impact your child's belief systems have on their outcomes. An important part of those belief systems is what they believe about themselves. Their beliefs about themselves are called self-image and self-esteem.

Self-esteem is undisputedly the most important factor determining your child's success or failure in every aspect of their life. How they view themselves determines their confidence and ability to function in social situations. It influences what goals they set and how much they believe in and work toward accomplishing their goals. It changes who they hang out with and how well their internal values compete with their desire to fit in. Self-esteem is their armor against all the negative messages and destructive influences in our society. It protects them against drugs, alcohol, delinquency, and unhealthy relationships.

ESPECIALLY KIDS WITH ADD

Low self-esteem is an issue with almost all kids, but kids with ADD are especially vulnerable. Each time they show up to class without their assignment, a small piece is chipped away from that armor. When they are singled out in class for talking out of turn, getting out of their seat, or not hearing the last instruction, another piece is chipped away. Getting their behavior card turned over, having to miss recess, getting sent to the office; these all damage their shield of self-esteem.

Perhaps most damaging to a child with ADD are the darts and arrows flung at them by their peers. When they hear things like "You're such a dork," or "retard," or "space case," these all hurt and leave small holes in their self-esteem. When the whispering stops as they walk up; when the invitations are passed out and pass them by; when they are the butt of a joke or even mentally or physically bullied, it can leave gaping holes in their self-esteem.

And after all that, they still must face the most dangerous battlefield of all: the one that will either annihilate what is left of their self-esteem, or provide a refuge, a haven where they can rest and repair and rearm. That place is their home. If the slaughter continues at home, they will lose hope.

A study I recently read on resilience showed that if a kid experiences negative attacks in every area of their life (home, school, and social settings), throughout the day (morning, midday, and evening), and over a prolonged period of time (weeks, months, or years), their resilient spirit will die. When it does, they will give up and give in to the destructive influences around them. ADD is a tough foe. If our kids lose their resiliency it will create a hole, which they will try to fill with self-medicating, self-destructive behavior.

I'll share with you this rather extreme case of what threatens the self-esteem of children with ADD. When my daughter was fourteen she volunteered to coach a soccer team made up of eight- and

---

Self-esteem is undisputedly the most important factor determining your child's success or failure in every aspect of their life.

---

nine–year-old boys. I went along as her assistant coach/mentor. She was doing a wonderful job except for managing one particular kid with hyperactive/impulsive-type ADD, whom I'll call Ted. I took on the challenge of keeping Ted's attention and energy focused on soccer. His mother was grateful and apologetic. I explained to her that because of my own ADD, I understood and didn't mind.

During one practice I started to send Ted for a lap around the field to burn off some energy. He was the fastest runner on the team and loved to show it. Just then a father of one of the other players stepped onto the field, and in a voice to be heard by all the players and parents, he said, "I am tired of this. ADD isn't real. It is just an excuse for bad parenting." I looked over at Ted's mother, who was probably doing more and better parenting than anyone present. Her head was lowered in embarrassment. I looked at Ted. He was finally calm; it was as if the man's words had hit him in the gut, knocking the wind out of him. I looked at the man and simply said, "You're saying this to the wrong person. I grew up with ADD and happen to know it's real." He was smart enough at that point to be quiet and leave the field and keep his opinions to himself the rest of the season. The man was grateful once the games started that Ted had so much energy. He scored most of our goals that year. I believe Ted's self-esteem survived thanks to such an understanding and supportive mother and the chance he got each week to use his superpower of sprinting up and down the soccer field.

GUARDIANS OF SELF-ESTEEM

If we as parents are the guardians of our children's self-esteem, and I believe that to be true, how do we protect and rebuild it?

You have already learned about the very important first steps. As you do the things I have discussed so far, you will see a remarkable improvement in your child's self-esteem. It has been said that parents provide the mirror in which children see themselves. As your child sees your understanding, acceptance, and empathy, any negative opinions they have about themselves will soften and start to dissolve. When a glass casserole dish has its edges crusted with baked-on *au gratin,* it takes a lot of scrubbing to make it shine again. However, if you set it in a sink of warm soapy water you can come back later and simply rinse it clean. Your compassion will have that type of effect on any grime that has collected on your child's self-image.

If your son or daughter feels that they have to hide a part of themselves in order for you to love and accept them, their self-esteem is weighed down by those secrets. Your child has to feel comfortable coming home and telling you the worst thing that happened to them that day, and even the worst thing they screwed up. They have to feel free to tell you that they flunked the spelling test because they forgot to study and that they punched Jake because he was making fun of them. And, here's one I have some personal experience with. They have to feel free confessing that they had to scrape gum off the bottoms of the lunchroom tables for stealing Jell-O from the lunch line.

When and only when, they feel you understand life from their perspective and accept their emotional reaction to it, will they start to heal from their wounds and rebuild their self-esteem. Then, as their ally instead of adversary, you can help them devise solutions and strategies against their ADD challenges.

These challenges are forgetfulness, impulsivity, difficulty focusing, planning, prioritizing, managing time, and managing their emotions. They are formidable foes—ones that gang up on them every day with relentless attacks. With help and over time they will learn to hold their ADD in check, but only if they go into battle fully protected by a strong vibrant self-esteem and armed with well-conceived plans of attack. I discuss helping them formulate plans of attack in a later chapter. Boosting their self-esteem is a vital prerequisite.

EMOTIONAL TINTING

Why is self-esteem so vulnerable? Why do we have to work so hard to protect it? To answer that you have to understand how it is formed in the first place. It is a product of our perceptions of what happens to us; the key word being "perceptions."

One of the basic principles of NLP states that "The map is not the territory." If you look at a road map or a trail map, or even a detailed topographical map, and then look up at the actual roads and scenery the map represents, you will notice that the two don't look anything alike. Our perception of a scene in life is based only on our own knowledge and emotions. We are missing details of the scene such as what the other person was thinking and feeling and what beliefs were motivating their actions. A myriad of hidden conditions exist beyond our ability to interpret the physical and emotional environment from all perspectives.

Our self-esteem is a countless collection of these inaccurate maps and our emotions about each one. As our brain stores each memory it evaluates its importance based on its emotional intensity. If you have a bowl of cornflakes for breakfast your lack of emotion about the event will allow that memory to fade over the next few days. However, if you come downstairs and your mother has waffles on your plate topped with whipped cream and strawberries, you will remember much longer. Your brain rates pleasure fairly high on the emotional scale and in order to repeat that pleasure in the future it stores it in a more permanent, detailed, and accessible location in your brain.

Unfortunately our brain rates fear and pain even higher on the emotional scale than pleasure. It is programmed that way for protection and survival. The more dangerous you perceive a situation to be, the more permanent, detailed, and accessible your map of the experience will be. So, if you come downstairs and have to face a bowl of Malt-O-Meal full of lumps, and under fearful duress you spend the next two hours traumatically and tearfully choking and gagging your way to the bottom of the bowl, while your friends are out having a gay ole time riding their big wheels around in the cul-de-sac; well, you might not voluntarily eat another bowl of Malt-O-Meal for the rest of your life.

You also might associate that same risk of pain with any other hot cereal. The brain looks at new situations and generalizes data stored in these protective memories with characteristics of new or anticipated situations. In this way a few negative memories tend to infiltrate our attitudes about life like a virus. If we are hurt by a few relationships, we may avoid all relationships. If we disappoint a few people, we may hesitate to make any commitments. If we fail at enough endeavors, we may quit attempting to accomplish anything in life. If enough powerful negative memories accumulate in our brain, our remaining pockets of self-esteem slowly shrink into isolated corners and can eventually completely dissolve.

YOUR ROLE WITH REGARD TO YOUR CHILD'S SELF-ESTEEM

I now need to convince you of something that you might not want to hear and might resist believing. This topic is usually covered in books written for people who struggle with low self-esteem and quite intentionally left out of books targeting their parents. I think you can handle it. If it is hard to hear, don't turn away; I have good news to follow. For now I need to clarify your dominant influence on your child's self-esteem.

The Role of Genetics

I have heard some parents try to protect themselves from feelings of failure and guilt by claiming that how their child turned out was determined purely by genetics. They convince themselves that all their child's mistakes were preprogrammed in their DNA, and that nothing they did or didn't do, said or didn't say, had any effect on their child's behavior whatsoever. Once again, because you are reading this book, I am sure you are not one of those parents. Why read a book about parenting a child with ADD if you don't have at least a hope that you can have a positive effect on your child's outcome?

I'm not saying that genetics didn't have a hand in your child's ADD. In fact, researchers estimate that 80 percent of the kids with ADD have it due to genetic factors. Most of the other 20 percent have it due to events or influences outside of their parents' control. That means that although you can affect your child's self-esteem in either a positive or negative direction, you are almost certainly not to blame for them having ADD.

Geneticists are also working hard to determine the role DNA plays in which temperaments children start out with and how they change during various developmental stages. By studying one-to-three-year-old twins, who share identical DNA, they estimate that genetics is 40 percent responsible for determining a child's temperament. That indicates that environmental influences may carry 60 percent of the weight. We as parents are responsible for that environment.

The Role of Parents

As a parent of six, I also concede that you cannot directly control most of the choices and behaviors that determine a child's path. However, whether you like it or not, you do directly influence their beliefs about themselves, and that indirectly sways every choice in either a positive or negative direction.

Experts identify early childhood interactions with parents as by far the biggest influence on a child's self-esteem. If a child feels safe and secure in their relationship with their parents, if they feel valued and loved, they will most likely develop a healthy level of self-esteem. If they feel physically or emotionally threatened, they will assume that something about them is wrong or bad. If they feel physically or emotionally neglected or abandoned, their feelings of

---

Experts identify early childhood interactions with parents
as by far the biggest influence on a child's self-esteem.

---

self-worth will take a huge hit. The younger they are and the more intense their feelings are, the more damaging these perceptions will be, and the harder it will be to change their patterns of self-talk and their self-defeating or self-destructive behavior.

Our parenting responsibility is sometimes a heavy burden to carry, especially when we feel we have harmed our child in the past. For some it creates guilt that lasts a lifetime. It doesn't have to. You have to cut yourself the same slack I'm asking you to cut them. You did the best you could, based on who you were and what you knew. Some mistakes you made because you didn't know a better way. At other times you knew a better way but your beliefs and conditioning kept you from acting on that knowledge. The only thing you can do at this point is apologize to your child and commit to them and yourself to learn and work to improve how you interact with them. Don't let past mistakes slow you down. Use them as motivation to move forward. If you understand and put into action what is in this book, I guarantee that your best effort will get better.

HERE IS THE GOOD NEWS

Damage to self-esteem is rarely irreversible. Some experts claim that it is never permanent no matter how severe. Negative memories can be changed. They can be reframed and relocated in the brain so that they lose their negative influence on self-esteem. Some tough ones are resistant to change. You may need to enlist the help of a therapist or life coach that specializes in just that. If you discover you or your child have some resistant memories that are stifling your self-esteem, don't hesitate to get help.

Damage to self-esteem is rarely irreversible. Some experts
claim that it is never permanent no matter how severe.

Let me use an experience with my youngest son as an example
of reframing negative memories. When he was about six we drove
down to my uncle's cattle ranch to help with roundup. While I was
off throwing calves in the corral my teenage daughter decided to
take him for his first horseback ride on the back of her horse. The
horse startled and they both fell off. Because my daughter was not
severely injured and had recorded enough other pleasant memories
of horseback riding, this singular experience did not taint her feelings about horses. My son, on the other hand, fell a long way from
his six-year-old perspective. He landed on his shoulder causing a
greenstick fracture in his collarbone—an extremely painful condition. He spent three hours on my wife's lap as we bounced over the
rough dirt roads between the ranch and civilization. As you may
have guessed, the painful experience left him with a fear of getting
on horses.

Now let me tell you the good ending to the story. It illustrates
how we can change the way we store a memory, not the memory
itself. Eight years after my son's horse-riding accident we were at a
family reunion at a ranch in New Mexico. At the age of fourteen his
fear of horses was still intact. After much patient persuasion, I convinced him to go on a slow, easy trail ride. I tried to make the situation as safe for him as possible, finding him the calmest horse and
assuring him he could turn back at any point. At first he simply sat
on the horse, subdued by fear, not knowing whether he would go or
not. Finally he decided to try. Along the way he started to relax and
I encouraged him to try a few things. Before the end of the one-hour
trail ride he was racing his horse up and down hills and across

streams. He was riding it like it was one of the four-wheel all-terrain vehicles he had grown up on.

All he needed is the same thing your son or daughter needs: a safe environment (you being patient, understanding, accepting, and empathetic) and the opportunity to feel some success. Practicing the actions outlined in this book will affect how your child perceives and records new experiences. Those new recordings will do much to mute or even alter ones that were previously recorded in a negative, emotionally charged way. Your child will also start to paint positive perceptions about your role in their life, which over time will recolor the negative ones. In all but the most difficult cases, these steps are enough to rebuild their self-esteem and free them to progress in life.

THE LANGUAGE OF SELF-ESTEEM

I can't leave this discussion of self-esteem without stressing the importance of language. How we view ourselves starts in feelings and emotions about experiences in our lives. Those feelings become anchored by how we talk about ourselves. Unless we quiet our inner critic, our boat will forever be anchored to those feelings, instead of sailing on toward our dreams.

Again, here is some bad news. Experts agree that a child's inner critic usually mimics their parents' voices. How you talk to your child will be how he or she talks to themselves for years to come. There is one sad exception to that truth: they will minimize or let go of the good statements you make and amplify and hold tight to the

---

Your child's inner critic usually mimics their parents' voices.
How you talk to your child will be how he or she talks
to themselves for years to come.

---

bad ones. That is why some parenting gurus say our children need to hear ten compliments to every one criticism. If you criticize them now or talk to them in demeaning terms they will develop what psychologists term the pathological critic. Without going into why their beliefs sustain such a negative alter ego, I will give you some tips on how to quiet it.

OUTSMARTING OUR INNER CRITIC

The first step in outsmarting our inner critic is to pick apart its logic. Following is a list of the most common fallacies it tries to perpetuate and the language it uses with each one. You need to become very familiar with these and recognize when it is trying to deceive you. Write them on an index card and keep them in your hip pocket. Get your child to help you make a poster of them and hang it in the place you most often talk. As you talk with your child watch vigilantly for the first sign of the critic in either their language or yours. If you hear it from them, chances are they heard it from you first.

Overgeneralization

The inner critic will take one instance and generalize about a person's entire nature. If your child fails once, the critic will tell them they can never do anything right. If one person doesn't like them, the critic will say that nobody likes them. Sadly, since the critic lives inside us, we have a tendency to try and prove it right. We start to sabotage our success and undermine our relationships.

Watch for words like never, always, all, every, none, no one, nobody, everyone, and everybody. Adhere to the common mantra, "Never say never."

If you catch yourself or your child using this false logic, restate the problem more accurately. Instead of saying, "You always lose your homework," state the specific frequency and situation, and how many times it wasn't true. You might say, for example, "You forgot your math homework twice this week. How many times did your remember it?" That will turn down the volume on the critic. It will also give you a measure for improvement.

Name-Calling

The critic likes to use the negative stereotypes created by our society. It's a fast, easy way for it to pack a lot of disrespect into a single word. Name-calling is overgeneralization on steroids, because it refers to your entire being, not just one area of your life. Sometimes the critic disguises its insults by making them sound like self-deprecating humor. There is a difference. Self-deprecating humor says that you did a silly thing; name-calling says that you are a silly person. If we hear these labels from others, we don't have to believe them. Unfortunately, we tend to always believe our inner critic.

Watch for pejorative terms like nerd, dummy, loser, joke, space case, or retard. The list is unlimited.

Make a list of the ones you or your child use. Write them on a piece of toilet paper and then flush them down the toilet. Smile and wave good-bye as part of your critic swirls into the stench of the underworld where it belongs.

Negative Filtering

The critic can be very one-sided in its observations. It tends to only notice and tell your child about the things they do wrong, and it will keep bringing them up until your child shuts it up. It never seems to notice their successes. My son had a high school basketball coach like that. He hit eighteen straight free throws during the season without a word from this coach. Finally, my son's streak ended with two misses and he heard about it for a week.

Watch for an unbalanced ratio of pointing out mistakes verses recognizing effort, progress, and successes. Monitor both you and your child.

Find every excuse to accurately compliment your child's efforts. If they mess up a couple of times, remind them of the eighteen straight other things they did right. Your child has to fire their critic as their coach. They will play much better without it.

If you think this one may be a problem for you but you aren't sure, get an index card and write the word negative on one side of it and the word positive on the other. Keep it in your hip pocket during the day. Make a check mark on the appropriate side as you listen to the language you use with your child. If you have problems remembering to listen, get in the habit of taking the card out of your pocket and holding it in your hand each time you come in contact with your child. If they ask you about the card, feel free to explain it to them. You can even give them permission to remind you to get your index card out at the beginning of a conversation. They will love that, and it will tell them how important they are to you, and show them a great example of how to attack a personal challenge.

Polarized Thinking

The critic also doesn't like to sit in the middle; it tends to see the world in black and white, right or wrong, winner or loser. It demands perfection, or else. To it, not being the best means you are the worst. One loss makes your child a loser. One sin makes them a sinner. Since no one can be right all the time, the critic sooner or later puts your child on the losing side. If your child believes this myth, they will be hesitant to work toward any goal. If one mistake equals utter failure, it puts the odds of utter failure too high to even try. Perfection is a myth that we must not buy into. Progress needs to be our only objective.

Watch for phrases like "I can't," "What's the use," or "Why bother."

The way to dispel this myth is to focus on progress. Help your child look back in time at where they were a month ago, a year ago, or even longer. Identify any progress that resulted from any efforts they put forth during that time frame or from merely staying in the game. Ask them, "If you have come that far in one week (month, or year), where do you think you'll be a week (month, or year) from now?"

Self-Blame

The critic wants to make your child feel responsible for everything bad that happens around them. If you are having a bad day, somehow it is their fault. If parents fight, somehow they are the underlying cause. If someone picks on them at school, somehow they provoked it. If a friend quits hanging out with them, they are 100 percent responsible. Taking responsibility for our actions is important. Taking responsibility for other people's action makes our self-esteem vulnerable. It becomes dependent on people and things outside of our control.

Watch for incessant apologizing, over sympathizing, or negative mind reading.

This one is sometimes tough to sort out. You have to be careful not to throw away personal responsibility when dumping false blame. The key is not to mind read; most of us are really bad at it. The critic wants you to assume that another person's negative thoughts are about you and because of you. The solution is simple. If you think someone is upset by something you did or said, just ask them. If you were the cause, you have a chance to apologize and make recompense, which will get it off your mind and theirs. If you were not the cause, you get to dump a big chunk of unnecessary self-blame.

Your child may have a hard time asking what is behind someone's emotions. Make it safe for them to practice on you. Explain to them that if they ever think you are upset at them, they can ask you what's wrong. Be honest in your answer. If you are upset about something else, you don't have to burden them with the details. Just assure them that they weren't to blame. If their behavior has upset you, explain accurately how their words or actions made your feel. Then assure them that your love for them was never in jeopardy.

Relational Thinking

The critic loves to compare. It compliments you based on someone else's failure. It criticizes you when someone else succeeds. Everyone is never as good as some folks and never as bad as others. If self-esteem is based on being better than others, it is doomed. How you feel about yourself becomes dependent on who you are with. Sooner or later you will run into someone who is better than you. Some people even downgrade their circle of friends in order to feel better about themselves.

Watch for any comparisons or a focus on what other people have or achieve.

The only person your child should compare themselves to is their past self. Are they making progress? Is their effort making them better today than they were last week, last month, or last year?

When my youngest son started school he came home one day and said that the boys had all raced at recess and that he was the fastest kid in his grade. Each year he would test his speed against the other boys. If some kid on the playground thought he was fast, my son would challenge him to a race. After each race he would come home beaming and report that he was still the fastest. In seventh grade I watched him compete at cross country against a kid who set a new school record almost every time he ran. To help him adjust to constantly coming in second place, we focused on his progress—each time he competed his times got better. We also focused on the other benefits of his efforts—he was getting into great shape for the upcoming basketball season. By the end of the season he had put himself on the record books with one of the top ten best times in school history.

Emotional Reasoning

Emotional reasoning is a dangerous circle of logic in which the critic tries to snare you. It will tell you that because you feel down, your life must be hopeless. Everyone feels down sometimes, but the critic tries to convince you that only losers feel discouraged. It wants to trap you in that negative emotion and take you as low as it can

You may feel down because you made a simple mistake. It is a natural response. If you cut someone off in traffic and they angrily honk their horn and gesture rudely, most people feel terrible for a few minutes. The critic will zero in on that natural emotion and tell you it is wrong to feel it. At some point you are no longer feeling bad about your mistake; you are feeling bad about feeling bad. If you stay with that thinking long enough you become depressed. Over time you may no longer recall what triggered your initial bad feeling. The critic will then tell you that because you are depressed for no good reason, you must be seriously flawed.

This is a dangerous path for anyone to go down. It leads to feelings of hopelessness that can prompt destructive behavior and even suicide. People with ADD are more susceptible to sustained emotions. They often have trouble recognizing their emotions in the first place. When they do recognize an emotion they tend to hyper-focus on it instead of rationalizing it and letting it naturally dissipate over time.

In its early stages you can help your child break out of this downward cycle by helping them identify and reframe the event that created their original negative emotion. Help them see the event accurately and in context. Validate that how they felt about the experience was natural. They will then be able to drop it off on the side of the road and not let it encumber the rest of their life.

If you suspect your child's critic has taken them too far down this path; if you sense they have ongoing feelings of hopelessness, please get professional help without delay.

POSITIVE WAYS TO BUILD YOUR CHILD'S SELF-ESTEEM

Quiet Your Own Critic

The first and most important step is to fire your own critic. If you hear any of the distortions I've talked about coming from you, stop yourself mid-sentence and correct your language. One person I know stops himself by saying the words "delete, delete," like he is hitting the backspace key on his computer. He then restates the same idea using more accurate language. Another person told me that she wears a rubber band on her wrist and snaps her critic whenever it gets out of line.

To me, "quieting the critic" is not harsh enough; I want to shut it up. Although the phrase "shut up!" was banned in our home, in this case I feel it is justified and appropriate. So I adopted a phrase from an entertaining commercial I saw. If I don't like what my inner critic is saying, I emphatically tell it, "Shut your big head up!" I immediately think I'm being shocking, bold, and funny, which is a positive self-image. It works every time.

If your critic has not yet learned to shut its big head up, make sure it at least knows it is not welcome in your interactions with your child. If it does show its big head in something you say to your child, correct it immediately in their presence.

If you hear its fallacies coming from your child, help them see themselves in a kinder, more accurate light. Have them tell you what they mean by, "I'm so stupid," or whatever they said about themselves. Once you have acknowledged their frustration, help them identify all the ways the fallacy they expressed about themselves isn't true.

Model Self-Esteem

You are not only the mirror of your child's self-esteem, you are their model—like it or not. Treat yourself with respect. They should see you taking care of your own basic physical needs, like proper diet,

> You are not only the mirror of your child's self-esteem, you are
> their model—like it or not. Treat yourself with respect. Stand
> up for yourself against abuse or injustice, be patient with
> yourself, and forgive yourself when you make mistakes.

rest and recreation, along with spiritual and emotional nourishment. Work to improve yourself through learning and trying new things. Especially in their early years your child sees themself as an extension of you. Seeing you invest in yourself will give them an innate sense of self-worth.

They should see you stand up for yourself against abuse or injustice, be patient with yourself, and forgive yourself when you make mistakes. Don't beat yourself up and act like you're the worst person on the planet. Talk about yourself and your appearance in an accurate and accepting manner. They shouldn't hear you say, "I'm so fat"; they should hear "I would feel better if I lost a few pounds."

Modeling healthy self-esteem will not only set the right example, it will put you in a calmer, more peaceful state to deal with the real child in the home. Not being stressed out or depressed will make you better at taking the positive steps outlined in this book.

If you have negative experiences in your past that are blocking your sense of self-worth, get help from someone trained in removing such blocks. If those experiences are part of your current environment, do what you can to eliminate them, for your sake and your child's.

Smiles

Smiles tell your child they are liked and thus likable. When you go for a while without smiling at them, they will assume it has something to do with them. If you are going through something that is affecting your mood, take a break from it occasionally. Sometimes that is hard to do, but try. Pretend you are locking it away in a drawer or sliding it under the bed. It will be there when you come back. Free yourself to face your child with a smile and a pleasant word. If you can do this as they are getting home from school or you are getting home from work, it will start the evening off on a positive note.

Hugs

Hugs tell your child they are safe and valued. They can be healing after a frustrating day at school or a turbulent experience with their peers. I wish I could go back and make up all the hugs I didn't give my kids. Some families are huggers, some are not. If your family is traditionally not a hugging bunch, traditions can be and often should be changed. Don't go overboard and hug them every time you see them. It will make them suspicious and seem forced. Don't announce one day that your new family goal is to hug three times a day. Make your hugs an appropriate response to a genuine feeling. Allow hugging to become a healthy part of your relationship.

Young children will normally be more naturally open to physical affection, whereas teenagers and young adults may have issues with you invading their personal space. If you haven't hugged them in a while, introduce the first one at a time when you are both feeling the corresponding emotional affection. If you still aren't sure they are open to it, simply ask, "Is it okay if I give you a hug?"

Time

Time tells your child they are important. Kids feel important when you spend time with them. They feel they are acceptable to be around. This may be something they have resisted in the past or even something you avoided because of problems in your relationship. After practicing the principles in this book, your relationship with them will change. It will become much more positive and will

---

Smiles tell your child they are liked and thus likable.

Hugs tell your child they are safe and valued.

Time tells your child they are important.

Free agency tells your child they are intelligent.

Responsibility tells your child they are powerful.

---

naturally draw you together. Let it happen. Make time for it to happen. Plan for it to happen. Look for common interests, maybe in one of their newfound superpowers. Even if it is not your superpower, you can be there to help them or just cheer them on.

Preserve some one-on-one time, but if they are having difficulty making friends, invite someone along. It will give you a chance to see them in action and learn where they are sabotaging relationships. It will also give you a chance to guide them and model healthy social interaction.

Whatever you spend time doing with them, make it a positive experience. Don't try to teach or coach. There is a time and place for those things. Sometimes you need to concentrate on just having fun and enjoying each other. If you are not in the right mood to be around them and you just can't get there emotionally, cancel. Tell them you just don't feel up to it this time and make it clear it is not because you don't want to be with them. Don't do this too often or they will assume it is them; however, it is better to postpone your time together than for it to be an unpleasant experience.

Free Agency

Free agency tells your child they are intelligent. Give them every opportunity to make choices. You as parent retain your veto power, but use it sparingly and justifiably. If it doesn't really matter, if it isn't dangerous or doesn't violate your moral code, let them decide.

Letting them call the shots gives them confidence in making decisions and gives them a sense of control in their lives. It also shows that you value their judgment and their individuality. If a certain decision comes up repeatedly, like which board game to play on Sunday afternoon, take your turn choosing. They will learn the valuable social skill of give and take.

Responsibility

Responsibility tells your child they are powerful. Have them decide which chores they want to do. Let them pick from a list of age-appropriate Saturday chores. They will feel a sense of accomplishment and that they are contributing to their own support. When they are done, take the time to inspect their work. Only hold them to an age-appropriate standard with a slight stretch added for growth and learning. If their work does not pass inspection don't judge them, simply coach them on getting the job done right. When you are both satisfied, celebrate all their good qualities that allowed them to do a great job.

Being responsible for a daily task such as taking out the garbage or feeding the dog taxes the memory skills of a kid with ADD. Discuss with them when the best time is to take care of the chore and ways to trigger their memory each day. It will take time and patience on your part, but don't give up—being able to establish a consistent routine is an important life skill.

Projects

I have found that kids will work hard and enthusiastically if they are by your side. At an early age I included my kids in as many of my projects as possible. If I was going to be relandscaping the backyard, I got them up early and asked them if they could help me. My needing their help was a great motivation for them. When they were very young the projects would sometimes take longer with their help than without. As they got older and I got older they could work circles around me.

Sometimes we would sit at the kitchen table the night before and plan out or design our project. They loved that time and felt invested in the work. They not only learned the fun of working hard, they learned to design, plan, solve problems, overcome obstacles, persevere and enjoy work. Most importantly they learned to value the feeling of proudly looking at the results of their efforts. What a boost to their self-esteem.

Don't Let Them Be Brats

Every kid has their moments when they act like a maniac, when they just become so emotionally upset that they go a little crazy. Most kids naturally learn that bratty behavior doesn't get positive feedback or results, and they learn more constructive ways to get what they want. A few kids adopt bratty behavior as their way of life, their identifying characteristic. They become bratty to the point that they know it, you know it, and everyone from the daycare center to the grocery store knows it. The impact this bad behavior has on their self-esteem is powerfully destructive.

Not only will they judge themselves for their bad behavior, people around them will judge them and treat them accordingly. Other parents won't want them to play with their kids. Even kids their own age won't want to be around them. When they walk into a room, they will sense with their little six-year old antenna that people feel they are bad. That is a sad situation; don't let that be your kid. Once they believe they are bad, they will act accordingly, which will further solidify their belief. It is a vicious, self-perpetuating, chicken-egg cycle that needs to be cracked.

Parents know when their child reaches that point, because they no longer like them. They still love their child and work and hope and pray that they get better. They feel guilty about their feelings, but they can't help looking forward to the time when their child is asleep or at school and they don't have to deal with them crying, yelling, hitting, throwing, disobeying, disagreeing, and destroying the house. This situation is sad for them and sad for their child. In spite of all the child's manic behavior, they will still sense their parents' mood. When they realize that their own parents think they are bad, their self-image will sink dangerously low.

I won't go into details here about how to put a stop to this cycle, because it is not the purpose of this book, but a lot of good books have been published on how to deal with kids throwing tantrums, throwing toys, kicking, biting, and spewing out, "I hate you" when things don't go their way. One book I particularly appreciated was *Have a Great Kid by Friday* by Dr Kevin Leman. The title is not an overstatement. Most children can learn good behavior very quickly when you make it in their best interest. Dr. Leman outlines a practical and effective step-by-step approach to stopping rotten behavior. They were steps my wife and I used on occasion that worked like a charm.

Also apply to the problem what you have learned in this book about acceptance and empathy. Acceptance will tell you that there is a rational need behind your child's irrational behavior. With your new empathy skills you will be able to identify what that need is and help them fill it in a more constructive way.

Just as ADD is a brain-based and not a parenting-based disorder, other related disorders such as Bipolar Disorder (BPD), Oppositional Defiant Disorder (ODD), and various Conduct Disorders (CDs) can make it difficult for a child to behave in socially adaptive ways. We know that with ADD, normal methods of organizing,

> Most children can learn good behavior very quickly
> when you make it in their best interest.

planning, and time management don't work. If normal methods of behavior management don't work for your child, you should seek a professional diagnosis, advice, and treatment. Just as with ADD, understanding the problem, making important parenting adjustments, and providing the right treatment can turn things around for a child struggling with a brain-based behavior disorder.

Embarrassment

That brings me to another important piece of advice. Don't discipline your child in public. If they are embarrassing you in public don't embarrass them back. Calmly take them outside or inside or wherever you can be alone and deal with the issue. Notice I said calmly—we've all seen arms practically removed from the socket in order to remove a child (or should I say "parent") from public embarrassment. Not only is that counterproductive, but these days it may prompt an anonymous call to child protective services.

This rule becomes even more important as they get older. To call your child out in front of their friends can sever your relationship. I made this mistake once with my daughter. I lost my patience with her in front of her friend. I knew better, but acted out of frustration. I immediately saw how hurt she was. I felt so bad that I gave her a red rose the next day along with my apology.

Apologizing

And that brings me to my final point about positively affecting your child's self-esteem. You will make some mistakes along the way, or you might be like me and make a lot of mistakes. Your kids know you aren't perfect. Don't pretend to be. An apology raises their self-worth. They feel more valued because you cared enough about their feelings and your relationship to do something most people find next to impossible—you sincerely apologized. Your son or daughter will witness an important example of how to acknowledge and deal with their own mistakes. Acknowledging mistakes is the first step in learning from them.

PRESS FORWARD

Don't be daunted by your unavoidable influence on your child's self-esteem. Now that you know what to do, practice and develop the skills to make that influence positive. You can do much to counteract the most destructive effects of your child's ADD: its constant erosion of their self-esteem. Years from now they will be telling someone that even though it was discouraging to grow up with ADD, you never quit believing in them. They will state emotionally that because of you, they never quit believing in themselves. You may even be the one they are telling that to, someday. How good will that feel? I'll tell you . . . it will feel terrific.

Provide Positive Motivation

GOAL 4

Now that you are helping your child understand and accept how their brain works, identifying their superpowers, and nurturing their self-esteem, the next ingredient is positive motivation.

They still have a long road ahead of them. In fact they may be dealing with ADD challenges their entire life, or until senility kicks in and then no one will know the difference. Even after they find their sweet spot, some elements of what they do will require them to compensate for their ADD. Some types of tasks will take them longer. Some goals will require them to get help. Sometimes they will fall on their face and have to back up and look for new strategies. To get through all of this they have to have a vision that drives them and a belief that they can ultimately reach their goals.

BELIEF = EFFORT

If your child doesn't seem motivated at school, they may no longer believe. We so commonly mistake their lack of effort for a lack of desire. All action is based on faith, or a belief that the result of that action will be successful or at least not painful.

When you go to climb a ladder you believe that particular ladder will hold you. If you didn't believe it, you wouldn't climb it. You may sit in a hole all day waiting for someone to help you out, with a perfectly good ladder standing there, mocking you. Passersby may look in at you and conclude that you are content in your hole. What they don't know is that the last three ladders you climbed collapsed, preventing you from climbing to your desired goal.

When it comes to school, your son or daughter may have had a few proverbial ladders give way on them and felt the pain of hitting the floor amid scattered shards. They may have even had a couple of splinters from that failure bite them in their backside.

I've seen that hesitation to try in many kids. It is not a lack of desire; it is a lack of belief. I ache for those kids. Their past is getting in the way of their future. Their potential is being obscured one disappointing failure at a time. At the same time I feel great hope for those kids. I can see their potential and know that belief can be restored by the reverse process, one success at a time. The same way your child generalizes their failures, they can generalize their successes. If they climb enough ladders without having them break and feel the satisfaction of reaching their goal, they will inevitably start to believe in ladders again.

Of course, anyone who fails at something and keeps doing it the same way will continue to fail. Your child may have heard quotes from people like Winston Churchill saying, "Never, never, never, never give up," and thought, "If I don't give up I will destroy what brains I have left by beating my head against this brick wall." Persisting in the face of failure is absolutely essential, but your child needs to learn the right way to persist.

> I've seen that hesitation to try in many kids. It is not a lack of desire; it is a lack of belief. . . . Their past is getting in the way of their future.

Your child has to be taught a new way of looking at their challenges and a new approach to solving them. That's what all your new learning about ADD will give them—new approaches, new strategies. Help them pick a challenge and guide them in mapping out a new way to attack it. If they fail, help them see their failure as another step toward their goal. Help them reevaluate their plan and make adjustments until they are satisfied with the outcome.

Applying these principles and reaching their goals will help them believe that eventual success lies at the end of any tough road. That is the belief they need; the belief that every problem has a solution; every challenge has a path to victory. They have to believe that obstacles, setbacks, and opposition, although part of the process, will not deny them ultimate success.

BORROWED FAITH

Sometimes a child doesn't have enough faith at the onset to try one more time. That faith can be borrowed from someone they trust. By following the steps outlined earlier in this book, you will become someone they trust. You have to believe for them. You have to look them in the eye and say, "I know there is a way to get to where you want to go. You might not get there on the first try, or even the second, but eventually, if we work together and keep learning and keep trying, you will get there."

If I had a child struggling with ADD who had run out of faith, I might tell them about all the amazingly successful people who have struggled through having ADD. Here are a few you may mention who have either a current or posthumous diagnosis of ADD: Michael Jordan, Michael Phelps, Will Smith, Jim Carrey, Albert Einstein, Bill Gates, Steven Spielberg, Walt Disney, John Lennon, John F. Kennedy, Dwight D. Eisenhower, and Abraham Lincoln.

These are only a few examples of the many people in this world who found their superpowers and didn't let their ADD stand in the way of being who they were meant to be. Learning about them helps me believe in my future. If they can achieve their dreams, perhaps I can achieve the vision that was planted in my brain, or at least I can achieve the goal that is in front of me today.

If your son or daughter is discouraged and afraid to dream and afraid to put forth their best effort, help them believe. Help them believe that life offers them the same opportunities as the next person. Help them believe that their ADD is not going to rob them of who they are meant to be. If they believe, they will keep searching for solutions; they will never give up; they will fight through until they become that person.

THE RIGHT GOALS

Start with Small but Yummy Bites

When a parent first introduces their toddler to baseball they don't take them to the batting cages, put a size-seven helmet on their head, hand them a thirty-ounce bat and shove them into a cage with the fast-pitch machine. If they did, their child would develop an understandable resistance to playing baseball. Instead, they go down to the toy store and buy a T-ball stand with a big plastic bat and a big soft ball. They place the ball on the tee and let them swing away until they eventually whack the ball across the yard. They then cheer and celebrate this simple achievement like they just hit a walk-off homer. Because of those first small but yummy bites of that child's baseball diet, they are likely to love the sport and want more and more. If that is where their child's talents lie, those parents may someday be cheering as they hit that homer in a real game.

> Help them develop an interest in the process of achievement and a renewed belief in their ability to succeed.

Your child may not understand goal setting at all at first. Give them a good taste of it up front. Make sure their first goals have a positive ratio of results to effort. Help them pick ones they can hit out of the park with just a few swings, and allow them to feel the thrill of victory. The first few goals don't have to fix a major problem or advance them toward a college scholarship. Your objective at first is to help them develop an interest in the process of achievement and a renewed belief in their ability to get what they want out of life.

Focus in on Their Passion

While you're doing all the great listening I discussed earlier, you will get a good idea of what they want to use their superpowers to achieve, change, overcome, or improve. Start bouncing this feedback off them until you find one or two goals they are passionate about. Although turning their homework in on time every day for a week may be the ideal goal, you need to also include a fun goal like being able to swim the length of the pool or make a new friend.

You may be worried that bringing home an A in math is not something they are passionate about. That time will come. They certainly don't enjoy struggling in math. Once they gain confidence at overcoming challenges and accomplishing goals, they will recognize their own desire to remove that negative from their life. By then they will not only be motivated, but they also will have the knowledge and skills needed to succeed.

HELP THEM SUSTAIN INTEREST

Interest Deficit Disorder

If your child is one of those who can sit and play a video game for hours on end, you know they can focus under the right conditions. If they play the same game day in and day out until every villain is wiped out and the final monster is annihilated, you know they can work relentlessly toward a goal that captivates them. So why can't they sit for fifteen minutes and study their spelling?

Recent research indicates that one face of your child's *attention deficit* is an *interest deficit* or what some call a *motivation deficit*. Your child may easily lose sight of why they want to learn their spelling words. They may not think ahead to the next day and picture themselves taking the spelling test with ease because of the time they spent studying the night before. They don't picture the scene where they hand you their report card and you praise them for the A in spelling and go on about their consistency in reviewing their spelling lists.

When I flunked geometry in ninth grade because of a zero homework average, it wasn't that I was rebelling against homework. I had great intentions of doing it but in the moment I wasn't compelled to do it. In the moment other activities like shooting hoops or riding my horse held more interest for me. In order to help your child succeed, you may have to deal with their sustained interest level. Following are some ways to make their goals more compelling.

Create a Vision

Once you identify a goal your child is interested in, how do you help motivate them to consistently take action? A vision is the next piece of the puzzle. Experts on achieving success are unanimous that having a vision is one of the keys to motivation. The people who advertise the video game your child loves understand this principle. They make it easy for kids to picture the ultimate goal of defeating the final monster or completing whatever quest the game presents. It remains a clear image in their mind the entire time they are playing. They may still think about it as they lie awake in bed and throughout the next day. By the time they get home from school they will be anxious to get back in there and go at it again. They know they won't beat the game that day, but that's okay. They visualize the

> Take a goal they feel some emotion about and
> help them visualize the end results. Once they
> believe it, they have to see it.

final outcome and how they will feel watching the horrid final toe fall to the ground. They are patient and keep at it day after day.

I won't lie and say that getting an A in math will ever compete directly with their video game; however, the game does have one weakness your child can exploit. They can remove it from the playing field by hitting the off switch when it's time to do homework. They can even put it on their side by using video game time as an incentive to completing their math homework.

Take a goal they feel some emotion about and help them visualize the end results. Once they believe it, they have to see it. You can start the process by saying something like, "What do you think that would be like?" "What do you think would happen if you accomplished that?" or "How do you think that would look and feel like?" Let them describe as much of it as possible. They need to be able to picture themselves in whatever winner's circle they want to be in. What will it look like? What will it sound like, smell like, taste like, and most important, feel like?

When the comedian Jim Carrey was struggling to get his career off the ground, he did something unique to help his vision be more real. Here's how he tells it:

> I wrote myself a check for ten million dollars for acting services rendered and dated it Thanksgiving 1995. I put it in my wallet and it deteriorated. And then, just before Thanksgiving 1995, I found out I was going to make ten million dollars for *Dumb & Dumber*. I put that check in the casket with my father because it was our dream together.

Isn't it encouraging that it was one of his parents who helped him maintain his dream of being a successful, highly paid actor?

Refill Your Child's Motivation Bucket

Kids with ADD are more likely to lose sight of a vision once they have it. No matter how excited they are at first, it tends to fade. The first two weeks of every semester I usually had straight As. I would burst through the front doors on the first day of school with a clear vision of the outcome. I could see how much my teachers would appreciate my conscientious effort. I could picture the look on my mother's face when I handed her my report card. But, before too long the vision of my future success would become sketchy until it didn't exist at all. Pretty soon I would forget to study for a test, not be paying attention when an assignment was given, or be too distracted in the evening to devote my time to schoolwork. As my vision faded my motivation faded. As my motivation faded my focus and discipline dissolved and my schoolwork went downhill in a hurry. I call this tendency to lose motivation over time the leaky bucket effect. I can fill my bucket with water but as I walk down the path toward my goal my motivation gradually leaks out.

Since I haven't yet found a way to plug my motivation leaks, the only solution is to periodically top off my bucket. In nonmetaphorical terms, I need to constantly refresh the vision of my end result. Sports teams sometimes do this by placing a picture of the trophy in the locker room. As they suit up for each game they think about how great it will feel to have the real one sitting there.

One tool experts in the field of achievement use to refill the leaky bucket is a vision board. A vision board can be as simple as a poster board covered in pictures and words that depict how the end result will look and feel. The pictures can be cut from magazines or found online. It can be a fun activity for you to help them with. Help them make it as accurate as possible and as emotion-invoking as possible.

Have them place their vision board in a conspicuous place, where they can see it when they wake up in the morning and when they go to bed at night. If their vision pertains to schoolwork, have them keep it where they can see it as they sit down to do their homework.

Your Child's Non-ADD Mind

Another powerful result of keeping their vision in the forefront of their mind is that it will release the power of their subconscious mind. *Their subconscious mind, by the way, does not have ADD. It can focus, plan, and organize quite well.* When I put my subconscious mind to work, it easily comes up with solutions that my conscious mind has fretted with. I don't know how many times I have put a problem out of my head and a day or two later, without any prompting, my subconscious mind hands me a clear, well-conceived solution.

Your child's vision board is going to put their non-ADD subconscious mind to work. It will solve problems for them, help them get over hurdles, formulate the right things to say, the right ways to organize, the correct choices to make, and the proper priorities to set. It will even help manage their time and emotions if those things are getting in the way of achieving their vision. Their subconscious mind will work all day and all night to get their real life to match their imagined life.

Recognize What Keeps Them Going

Different things motivate different people. Some children aren't captivated at all by video games or vision boards. Look for things that capture and hold your child's attention. Look for activities they can do for hours without becoming bored or tired. Analyze what about that activity compels them. Use it as a model to sustain motivation toward productive goals.

The summer after my third grade year something engaged me so completely that I became a hermit. My mother was a puzzle lover. Santa Clause had dropped off one or two thousand-piece puzzles every Christmas for years. The first day of that summer vacation I started working one on the linoleum floor in our den. Two weeks later I had worked every puzzle we owned, so I simply put them away, went outside, and spent the rest of the summer exploring the pastures and ponds of my rural East Texas stomping grounds.

When, as an adult, I was looking for ways to sustain motivation, I thought back on that experience. I realized that watching the picture in a puzzle slowly reveal itself and the pile of pieces slowly dwindle drove me to find one more piece. I realized that I am easily captivated by watching steady progress. I have been able to apply that point of self-awareness to daily motivation.

If I can create a way to visually track the effects of my daily effort, I can go virtually forever without my motivation bucket running dry. I was once in a training program which required me to read thirteen books. Being a fairly slow reader, the assignment was daunting. I made a chart of the chapters of each book and stopped after each chapter and filled in what percent of the book I had completed and how many hours of reading I had left. I was surprised by how driven I was each day to return to my reading. I finished every book before its deadline, much like the way I finished those thousand-piece puzzles. Using a simple observation about my own nature, I had devised a powerful strategy to maintain my motivation.

REWARDS

Intrinsic vs. Material Rewards

The use of rewards or incentives is the second of the two most debated issues in the treatment of ADD. Most professionals debating pro-rewards site both clinical and anecdotal evidence that offering immediate and consistent rewards is an effective way to motivate children to change their ADD behavior. Simply put, dangling a dollar bill or banana split can have an immediate positive effect on a child's actions.

The concern of some is the long-term effect reward systems will have on your child's ability to be self-motivated. They worry that motivating good behavior with immediate material rewards inhibits your child's development of more intrinsic motivation. They fear that it will create a "What's in it for me, now?" attitude and that your child will be less prone to focus on the immediate good feeling and the long-term benefits of doing the right thing for the right reasons.

Professionals arguing the side of material rewards have observed that as some children feel the positive effects of doing the right thing for a material reward, those positive feelings alone eventually take over as their primary motivation.

I won't argue for one side or the other, but only advise you, as I did with the issue of medication, to listen to both sides of the debate and then follow what you feel is the best fit for your child based on their unique personality.

Different children respond very differently to the various types of incentives. For the most part my children have been completely unaffected by the opportunity to earn material rewards by behaving a certain way. They have seemed offended by the manipulative nature of the offer. Perhaps it told them that I didn't trust them to do the right thing on their own.

Positive Reinforcement

All children seem to respond positively to rewards given after the fact to recognize effort, celebrate progress, or simply reinforce positive behavior. Every child has an innate desire to please their parents or the parent figure in their life.

The need for parental approval is driven by an even deeper need for self-acceptance. If we nourish them with a regular diet of praise

> If your child can't satisfy their hunger for approval at home,
> they will be driven to forage for it with friends.

and recognition, it will satisfy that hunger and reduce their appetite for external approval. Their main motivation will shift from a desire to please their parents to a need to be true to their own positive self-image.

An important side effect will be that their motivation will be less attached to a desire to please the world. In more relevant terms, they will be more immune to peer pressure. If your child can't satisfy their hunger for approval at home, they will be driven to forage for it with friends. It will eventually become like an addiction, a controlling factor for their behavior, and without conscious awareness it may carry them to places they never intended to go.

Helping Your Child Move Forward

SECTION FOUR

Are You Ready?

The steps you have read up to this point in this book will not solve your child's ADD. They merely put you and your child side by side on the right path to solutions. They prepare you to move forward together on that path, with fewer emotional detours.

At this point you may be ready for the actual solution. If you understand and feel the importance of each step I have laid out and you are committed to and engaged in doing them, you are ready to focus on forward progress. You don't have to have completely mastered any of them; none of us ever do. You just have to understand, value, and commit to them. If you are there, read on. If you are not there, what I will tell you in this section will result in more frustration for both you and your child.

If you are ready, here is the *process of forward motion* in one simple statement: When your child sees something positive they want to accomplish but their ADD seems to be standing in their way, help them (1) define a goal, (2) brainstorm strategies, (3) formulate a plan, (4) work the plan, and (5) evaluate the results. Then simply help them repeat these steps until they reach their goal.

THE POWER OF A PROCESS

If the mere mention of the words *process* and *planning* causes a slight panicked feeling to creep into your mind, I understand. Like me, you may not be a natural planner or project manager. Don't let that stop you from reading on. I have tried to simplify the process as much as possible while still including all the essential details. Like me, you may find that your brain can handle more complex tasks if the process is clearly outline.

As your child visualizes their end result, you will see the excitement rise in them. If they are anything like me, when they get excited about doing something, they want to jump up and run out immediately and start getting it done. They want to skip the up front steps that ensure their success. You know that without those steps things will not go well. If things don't go well enough times, your child will eventually become discouraged and want to quit.

Again, their beloved video game is a great example of following steps to a goal. Mario can't just go rescue the princess. He first has to eat a couple of mushrooms to prepare himself for the dangers along the way. He also has to find the extra lives and gather enough coins so that if he gets hit by an axe-wielding turtle, he can bounce back. Once he is well equipped, he has to progress through each world and finally, after he has slain all the intermediate monsters, he can face his final foe and rescue the princess.

(Sorry that my video game example is so outdated, but *Super Mario Brothers* is the last video game I mastered. After two solid weeks of around-the-clock effort to rescue the princess, my wife simply told me, "Don't ever do that again." For the sake of my marriage and my own mental health I have complied.)

Do you see what video game creators know, that you and your child need to know? They lay out a process that leads to success. They also do what in the ADD coaching world is called "chunking." They break the project down into intermediate steps that can be

> When they get excited about doing something, they want to
> jump up and run out immediately and start getting it done.
> They want to skip the up front steps that ensure their success.

accomplished in a fairly short amount of time. They build into the game intermediate achievements along the way so that a feeling of accomplishment and belief is sustained during the lengthy quest. When your child persists after multiple defeats and develops the particular skills needed to make their avatar jump from one moving platform to the next while avoiding flying piranhas, they are filled with a great sense of achievement. When they finally beat the first level of the video game, they feel like they are on their way. They feel that with enough focus and effort they can reach their ultimate objective. This chapter outlines how to help your child beat each challenging level in their game of life.

LET THEM DRIVE

It was my job and enjoyment as a dad to teach each of my six kids how to ride a bicycle. During that process I always kept my hands off the handlebars. I held on to the back of their shirt so I could give them just enough support while they gained their sense of balance. I held on loosely so that they could feel the effects of their actions. They felt how their bike reacted if they quit steering or they stopped pedaling. As they gained more skill, I loosened my grip until I eventually had no effect on them at all. When I was ready to let go completely I gave them this advice. "It will take five ouwies to master riding your bike." Each time they fell and scraped their knee or their hand I acted excited that they had gotten one more ouwie out of the way. None of them made it to five.

As you help them reach their goals remember these basic rules:

- Hold on loosely

- Let them steer

- Have them move forward under their own power

- Celebrate their mistakes as a necessary part of mastering
  a new skill

Define
the Right Goal

STEP 1

POSITIVE VS. NEGATIVE GOALS

Your first brainstorming session needs to be spent deciding on two goals to work on first. Having a balance between positive goals (ones that build positive skills and habits) and negative goals (ones that fix or eliminate problems) is a simple concept, but an all-important principle.

One Building Goal

Your child's first goal should focus on developing a skill or talent from their growing list of superpowers. Progress in a positive area in their life will do wonders for their confidence and motivation when it comes to eliminating negatives. You will be amazed how something like entering a pencil sketch in the city art contest will change how they feel about the rest of their life. It won't be an instant fix to every problem; they won't suddenly overcome their ADD, but they will start to know themselves better, esteem themselves higher, have more hope for their future, and be calmer, more confident, and willing to improve other areas of their life.

One Fixing Goal

Because your child has ADD they will probably have no problem coming up with a list of problems to address. It is compiled from all the times they have been scolded, lectured, singled out, left out, ridiculed, punished, or picked on. Because you both now understand and accept how ADD affects their life, they should be willing to discuss these problems openly and select one to address.

Help them identify what is causing them particular discomfort or frustration in life. Look at specific areas like homework, recess, friends, siblings, the morning routine, or the afterschool soccer practice. If they don't happen to pick the one issue that is top on your personal list of discomforts, you can mention it in the context of brainstorming, but don't try to sell it. If you do, they will feel your hands on the handlebars and turn the entire process over to you.

A LIMIT OF TWO

Resist selecting more than one building goal and one fixing goal. That doesn't mean other worthy accomplishments should not be pursued or effort should not be put toward overcoming problems. Goals are unique in that performance is measured with an expectation of progress and improvement. That expectation should create just enough stress to compel them to action without overwhelming them. Too much stress will stop most kids in their track and cause some to rebel and act out. It simply sets them up to fail.

Let me reemphasize, however, that when your child sees progress in their first two goals, their accomplishment will send positive ripples across their pond, affecting every aspect of their life.

MIX IN SOME QUICK WINS

Children with ADD need to be constantly encouraged by their own forward motion and frequent celebrations. Especially at first help your child pick some goals they can accomplish in a matter of days. They need to get an initial feel for how the process works and how good it feels to move forward under their own power. They can also taste victory in the form of the hot fudge sundae you promise them as an incentive. If they ever seem reluctant to set goals, help them find another quick win. It can even be a smaller chunk of a larger goal.

TURNING WISHES INTO GOALS

Help your child turn each goal into a real goal, not just a wish. They do this by adding the two essential elements of a real goal: a measurement and a deadline.

For example, instead of having a wish of getting along with their sister, they could set a goal of going one whole week without teasing her. Kids need to see a concrete, measureable end point they can work toward. They may also need more help deciding what that end point is.

Measurements

Help them add measurability to their goal by asking open-ended questions:

- What would give you a feeling of accomplishment?
- What would make a real difference?
- What would be worth celebrating?

Some kids' answers will reflect a lack of faith in themselves based on their past performance. If they only think they can go one day without teasing their sister, that's okay for now. Once they reach a couple of lower rungs on the latter, they will start to believe and continue to climb.

Other kids are eternal idealists and will only see the top rung. If they think they can go the rest of their life without teasing their sister, that's okay, too. It is great to be an idealist as long as you create intermediate goals to keep yourself motivated. Help them identify the individual rungs on the climb to their goal. They can set a deadline to tally up their teasing each night or each Sunday. The important thing for now is to create a way to measure progress and success.

Deadlines

If your child struggles with a poor awareness of time, they will need lots of help setting a deadline for certain types of goals. If someone at the office ever asked me when I would have something done, I had three pat answers. Favors took two minutes, tasks took two hours, and projects took two weeks. These answers set my bosses and coworkers up to be either impressed and appreciative or disappointed and frustrated—usually the latter. Setting deadlines was always a roll of the dice with the odds stacked against me. I learned that I was better off doubling my most thought-out time estimate or deadline.

BELIEF AND MOTIVATION

Once they have a solid goal, put to use what you have learned about belief and motivation. Have a vision board party where you create a new vision board just for this goal. You can make it out of letter-sized construction paper for simple goals or out of poster board for more complex goals. Gather a stack of magazines to cut pictures from, go to the internet for pictures and clip art, or have them draw pictures depicting their success and how it will feel. They can add meaning with captions, headings, or encouraging remarks.

Then have them place it where it will do the most good. If their goal is to get an A in math, their vision board should be hanging by where they sit to do their math homework. If their goal is to be able to run a mile without stopping, it should be next to their running shoes.

Brainstorm
Strategies

STEP 2

STRATEGIES BASED ON PRINCIPLES

Next, brainstorm with your child on what strategy you are going to use to solve the problem. An ADD strategy is simply an approach to accomplishing a task, which accounts for a common ADD symptom. They are based on a multitude of principles of self-management and achievement.

For example, if I had a goal of dunking a basketball, I might apply a principle I call incremental bar raising. My strategy might be to first touch the rim, then dunk a golf ball, then dunk a baseball, then a softball, volleyball, soccer ball . . . Well, you get the idea. The principle of *incremental bar raising,* teaches you to set incremental goals that help you stretch and encourage you to sustain effort toward a lofty goal. The strategy is how the principle is applied to a specific goal, problem, or challenge. In my example, the strategy was to increase the size of the ball until I reached my ultimate goal of dunking a basketball.

Here is a more relevant example applied to the common ADD symptom of not being able to get out of bed on time. You might guide your child to a strategy based on the self-management principle, *making it unavoidable.* Their initial strategy might be to set two blaring alarm clocks, one by their bed and one on the other side of the room to go off five minutes later. They might also apply the principle of *aligning your nature* by specifying that they must turn on a bright light when the first alarm goes off so that their own senses naturally nudge them toward wakefulness. They might even select a third strategy during the winter months based on the principle of *linking it to pleasure.* The third strategy could be to set the second alarm clock next to the hot shower, so they can reward themselves for getting out of bed with the awesome feeling of a hot shower on a chilly morning.

I can think of at least a dozen strategies just for getting up and going in the morning. The database of ADD strategies is overflowing. It includes systems, methods, and approaches to help your child get out the door in the morning and get to bed on time at night; get their homework done in the evening and get it turned in the next day; make new friends and get along with their enemies; pay attention in class and stay appropriately seated. As I continue to study how to deal with ADD, I am constantly amazed by the innovative strategies parents and professionals have devised to help children compensate for ADD in absolutely every aspect of their life. If you continue to study ADD, you will become a source of those strategies in your own brainstorming sessions.

BRAINSTORMING BASICS

One key to brainstorming is to get as many ideas on the table as possible before evaluating or prioritizing any of them. Set a quota at the beginning of the session to come up with at least five possible strategies. If your child throws out an idea, wait until the planning step to help them refine it. If they just can't come up with any strategies on their own, ask them if you can throw out a few options. Giving them choices allows them to remain captain of their own ship and keeps them invested in the process. When you come up with an idea, your child will try it on and think about how it fits. This may stimulate their creativity, which combined with their insider knowledge may produce just the right approach.

Another key to brainstorming is to prime the pump and get the creative juices flowing. Here are a few idea inspiring items you might have handy.

A Specific Goal

To begin with, be sure your child's goal is clear and in front of you during the session so that you don't veer off path.

Superpowers

Now would be a great time to pull out the list of your child's superpowers. It will trigger more and better strategies and ones that better align with your child's natural abilities—an important key to their success.

101 EDF STRATEGIES

The following list contains strategies you and your child can use as building blocks when tackling challenges with the executive functions discussed earlier in this book. It will be an important resource. If you get stuck in your brainstorming, read through the list and consider how each one could be applied to your child's goal or challenge.

Saying that this list is definitive would be like saying that all the great novels have been written. Someday, during a brainstorming session, you and your child will have a jolt of inspiration that will add another brilliant strategy or principle. When you have that stroke of genius, I hope you will share it with me. In fact, you can find an updated list of self-management principles and strategies at www.ADDParentingSupport.com.

Getting focused

- Clear your mind
- Deep breathing
- Verbalize your focus
- Review your purpose
- Review your last notes

Staying focused

- Control your environment
- Clear your line of sight
- Make up a game
- Jot main points
- Get a body double

Staying alert in boring situations

- Enhance the experience
- Rate yourself
- Take a snack
- Doodle

Planning

- Chunk it down
- Work backward
- Ask, "And then what?"
- Talk it through
- Answer the four Ws

Prioritizing

- Learn the details

- Create a timeline
- Ask, "What if I didn't?"
- Look for the one

Organizing

- Use what worked
- Keep it simple
- Make it natural
- Build it in

Starting an activity

- Visualize the outcome
- Pick just one
- Link it to fun
- Set yourself up
- Focus on the first step

Sustaining motivation

- Dream the dream
- Refresh your vision
- Invite a friend
- Track small progress
- Draft a contract

Transitioning between tasks

- Signal a distraction
- Put it away
- Relocate
- Reposition

Completing projects

- Create a punch list
- Allocate time
- Create an urgency
- Schedule a celebration

Managing time

- Egg-time it
- Calculate your pace
- Schedule blocks
- Define what's next

Remembering appointments

- Review your calendar
- Create triggers
- Set an alarm
- Stick a sticky note

Remembering lists or instructions

- Keep a quick-draw notepad
- Require it in writing
- Simplify the steps
- Post a list of steps

Establishing habits and routines

- Stage it ahead of time
- Put it in the way
- Define procedures
- Check it off

Turning off at bedtime

- Set TV and PC timers
- Eat light
- Save your reading
- List ways to relax

Turning on in the morning

- Move your alarm clock
- Hit the lights
- Plan your morning
- Hit the shower

Learning from past mistakes

- Be honest
- Get feedback
- Picture next time
- Tell your journal

Anticipating outcomes

- Ask, "What if I did?"
- Fast forward
- Rely on experience
- Ask someone else

Adapting to change

- Fake enthusiasm
- Explore the details
- Take a friend
- Find a mentor

Coping with chaos

- Cover it up
- Organize it
- Isolate a piece
- Take a break

Regulating emotions

- Reframe it
- Distract yourself
- Find the positive
- Talk it through

Managing frustration

- Ask for help
- Take a break
- Take a step back
- Brainstorm solutions

Monitoring nonverbal feedback

- Freeze frame a video
- Ask for the verbal
- Get a tutor
- Go to the movies

Inhibiting speech and action

- Count to three
- Make tick marks
- Anchor relaxation
- Switch to passive

Proven Strategies

Even more valuable would be a list of strategies that have worked for your child in the past. Those strategies become like convenient frozen entrées you can just pop in the microwave and are ready in minutes. If having sticky notes taped to the fridge has worked in the past make sure that strategy is handy by adding it to their list

Formulate a Plan

STEP 3

Step three is to help your child plan in more detail how they are going to implement their selected strategies. Strategies are their hows—defining their whos, whats, wheres and whens will give birth to a plan. As with the other steps it is important that you guide the process while letting them steer. You are not teaching them planning skills through example; you are empowering them by helping them practice those skills themselves.

COACHING QUESTIONS

Ask them the kinds of questions they will need to ask themselves when planning on their own. Don't press for an answer—your questions are only meant to stimulate the planning portion of their own brain. If they have steered the process up until this point, your questions won't seem like a verbal final exam.

Open-ended questions like the following will coach them toward formulating a robust plan:

- What details need to be added to this plan to give it the best chance of success?
- Who do you need to coordinate with to accomplish that?

- What will you need on hand to perform that task?
- Where would you be most likely to concentrate without interruptions or distractions?
- When would you be most affective doing that?
- What has tripped you up in the past and how can you eliminate it or steer around it?
- What would motivate you to follow through?
- What is the best way for me to support you in this goal?
- How can you make the plan more natural or automatic?
- Does the plan fit with other things you or your family has going?

MATURING THEIR PLAN

Of course a newborn plan is not capable of much. Your child needs a plan that is fully grown. Adding elements such as *chewable chunks, accountability, intermediate deadlines, rewards* and *simplicity* will give their plan the mature character it needs to succeed.

Chewable Chunks

Small chunks are much easier to chew and swallow. This point in planning is where you can help your child with a skill that the majority of kids with ADD lack, namely chunking things down into bite-sized pieces. The plan to reach a goal may seem to your child like a large, dark mist looming in their path full of unseen pitfalls and frustration. The more they try to see through the fog the darker it becomes and the more undoable it seems. The exercise of planning can freeze them at the starting line.

One of the great benefits of chunking is that you don't have to plan all the steps before you get going. Your child can focus on the first one or two and put the rest away while still keeping the end goal in mind. They can travel lighter by not having to worry about the next chunk until they are ready for it. Chunking is the best tool to facilitate action in a child with ADD.

Several methods exist to help with chunking:

- Work Backward — Envision the end goal and ask yourself, "What has to happen just before that?" Then you identify what has to happen just before that . . . and before that . . . and . . . well you get it. One of my mentors described it as picturing yourself walking down a mountain backward in order to know how to get to the top.

- And Then What — You identify the first and smallest step toward a goal, like putting on your shoes in the morning, and then you ask, "And then what?" You answer with the next step and then repeat the question until your next answer is, "Go celebrate!"

- Lean Into It — Sometimes it is better to only identify the next chunk or two. It is useful or even necessary when it is difficult to identify the steps toward a goal or to visualize how the final success will look. Sometimes you only know the direction you want to go. You just lean in that direction by determining what steps you can see and doing them. At some point in your doing, the next door opens and the next step appears from behind it. All you have to do is keep leaning into it and you eventually get there.

Accountability

Accountability is one aspect of your child's plan that especially needs to come from them. Talk to them about how some form of accountability will help them achieve their desired goal. Allow them to pick a form that they are comfortable with. If their choice involves reporting to you, have them initiate the report, not you. If you ask them for it, they may feel you are nagging. You can build in extra rewards for when they report to you without being prompted. They can also take an indirect approach to reporting by updating a chart or calendar with their progress or checking off a task list that is posted where you can see. Again, an extra incentive can be given when they update their progress without being prompted.

Set yourself up to be a cheerleader, not squad leader. When you cheer, make it about them. Echo their positive feelings of success, not yours. If you focus on your excitement, they may wonder how you are going to feel when they fail—especially if you have expressed your disappointment in the past.

When they don't succeed, focus on their disappointment and frustration, not yours. Unless they recognize their own discouragement, over time it may build into stress and then anxiety. Anxiety will almost always freeze them in their tracks. They need to learn to hold themselves accountable without letting small setbacks and mistakes slow them down.

Intermediate Deadlines

Imminent deadlines are a great source of motivation. Any success guru will tell you that a looming deadline is a great tool to focus your efforts. That tool sounds like a perfect fit for someone with an attention deficit. Even if your child's goal has a natural deadline such as the end of the grading period, have them focus instead on where they want to be when the first progress report comes out. If that is not immediate enough, most teachers will agree to send home a more frequent and more detailed report of how they are doing. A goal such as not teasing their sister doesn't have a natural end. They can create a false deadline by scheduling weekly or biweekly review sessions with you or even with their sister.

While training for her first marathon, my wife picked out a half marathon to run at the point in her training schedule when she should have been up to running that distance (about thirteen miles). The more imminent deadline made each training session seem more important. When she breezed through the half marathon she was encouraged that her training plan was working and that her timeline to reach her goal was reasonable. Each small success reinforced her belief that she could complete a marathon and motivated her to manage her regimen and face her next challenge.

Rewards

Rewards can be physical, monetary, or intrinsic in value. The more you tie them to real life the more they build character and prepare your child to be completely self-motivated. Monetary rewards may be effective for some children, but when you are an adult it is difficult to pay yourself in dollars for reaching goals when all your money is yours to begin with. However, as an adult you can dangle physical carrots in front of yourself like a trip to the spa, a date to the movies, or sitting down to watch a football game with a plate full of nachos.

Self-rewarding serves two purposes for someone with ADD. It is not only an incentive, it also interrupts the common ADD pattern of instant gratification. You only get football and nachos after the yard work is done. If you can help your child learn to motivate themselves by dangling their own carrots, you will be giving them a powerful tool to help manage their life.

Whatever intermediate rewards your child picks, they should also focus on the intrinsic rewards of accomplishing a goal. Their vision board will help them focus in that area. If they review it daily, they will be focused on how good it will feel to get an A in science, instead of the dollar that A will earn them. They will look forward to having a clean room every day, instead of the fifty cents they will earn for doing a minimal job of picking it up. They will grow to where earning good grades or living in a clean room is reward enough.

Simplicity

Simplicity is a key to any plan. Simply put, the simpler it is the more likely it will simply work. Once their initial plan is in place, help them look for ways to streamline it. Kids with ADD often have trouble remembering the steps of a complex procedure. Help them pare the steps down to three or four. If it must be more complex, ask them what strategy could help them remember and follow the process. In my life as a computer nerd I created checklists and job aids for any process I would have to periodically repeat. If I trusted myself to simply remember the steps they had to be very simple.

Making each part of the plan a more natural part of their daily routine can also simplify it. Instead of creating a new process, help them tie the process to some activity that already occurs. For example, instead of planning to feed the dog at 8:15, they can plan to feed Sparky when they get up from the breakfast table. That will give them a natural trigger so they won't have to set a special alarm.

EXAMPLE PLAN

Here is an example of a simple plan. If your child is getting their homework done but showing up at school the next day without it, their goal might be to turn their homework in on time for an entire week. They might incorporate their strategies into the following plan:

- "After I finish my homework, I will place it in my binder
  and then immediately put my binder in my backpack
  and immediately place my backpack by the front door."
  Strategy: Stage it ahead of time
  Plan includes: What, when, where

- "Today I will stick a note on the front of my notebook
  reminding me of these steps: 1. Binder, 2. Backpack,
  3. Report, 4. Snack."

Strategy: Define procedures

Plan includes: What, when, where

- "When I report to you that my homework is in my backpack, I can go in the pantry and get an Oreo cookie or fruit rollup. Your role is to always keep Oreos and fruit rollups in the pantry. If I reach my goal of turning it in on time for an entire week, I get to play NBA Jam for an extra hour during the weekend."

  Strategy: Link it to pleasure

  Plan includes: Who, when, accountability, reward

- "At the end of two weeks I'll tell you how I think the plan is working."

  Plan includes: Intermediate deadline

YOUR ROLE IN THE PLAN

Notice that your role in the plan is one of supporting their efforts. Try not to burden yourself with being involved in every step. Learn to be more of a one-minute manager than a micromanager. The goal here is for them to use their own strengths to tackle their challenges, not yours. They need to learn to pedal their bike hard enough to sustain balance and forward motion. Have you ever seen a kid's face the first time they ride their bike across the blacktop or swim the length of a pool all on their own? They beam with a feeling of power and self-confidence. Their self-worth and self-esteem are sky-high. That feeling will drive them where they need to go in life.

Work the Plan

STEP 4

Once your child is satisfied with their plan, let them drive it long enough for a thorough road test. If they are involved in brainstorming and planning they will take more ownership and want to work harder at making the plan succeed. They will also be more open to you coaching them just enough.

AUTOMATIZING

Kids with ADD, and adults with ADD for that matter, take longer and require more consistent and conscious effort to form a habit or internalize a process. The difficulty is in their ability to automatize actions; to reach a point where the minute actions of a task don't require deliberate thought. When we first learn to drive we have to consciously think through each step, but over time we get to where we can monitor traffic, signal to turn, change lanes, and alter speed, all while carrying on a conversation and adjusting the radio.

If someone has a hard time walking and chewing gum at the same time they can automatize it. By consciously practicing long enough they will eventually be able to do it without thinking. Musicians and athletes understand the results and benefits of committing a sequence of actions to their subconscious mind through conscious repetitive execution. They dedicate hours turning a rough rendition or awkward move into a flawless flow of an unconscious sequence of actions.

With ADD, automatizing may require more intentional effort, but over time difficult things will become simpler and more automatic. When that happens a piece of the framework that will support your child's success will be in place. Their self-esteem will grow under the knowledge of having become independent in one more area of their life. With a logical plan built upon solid strategies automatizing will happen by simply sticking to it.

CHEER AND MOTIVATE

Your biggest part in this phase is to ignore any failures and point out any slight improvement, progress, or effort. Remember that effort without progress equates to future progress if you learn from it. Look for any valid reason to celebrate incremental success while encouraging them to continue on to their goal. Be their cheerleader and promoter. When another family member walks into the room, ask them to guess what their son or daughter, brother or sister accomplished this week. Make each of your kids a frequent hero in your home. Don't worry; it won't go to their heads, at least not in a bad way. If they seem arrogant it usually indicates a negative self-image, not a positive one. The more you brag on them, the less they will feel the need to self-promote.

Continue to help your child sustain motivation by keeping the end result in mind. When celebrating small successes help them reload their vision of how it is going to feel when they reach their final goal. Review their vision board occasionally and ask them about particular pictures or captions. No matter how blaring their vision board is, over time it will start to blend into the paint or become part of the wallpaper.

Part of celebrating incremental successes could be to add a picture or caption to their vision board depicting their progress. Doing this will remind them of both their end goal and their steady progress. They will get a potent shot of confidence every time they look at it.

When my wife started training for her first marathon we made up a large poster with her running goals for the ten weeks leading up to the race. We hung it in our bedroom next to the door where we would most likely see it several times a day. Each day after her training run we drew some silly picture on it depicting a characteristic of that day's accomplishment. She never missed a beat. Ten weeks later she ran her first marathon in under four hours without stopping or walking. She even sprinted across the finish line. Much of her unwaning motivation and consistent effort was due to that poster.

Evaluate
the Results

STEP 5

After a reasonable amount of time and effort help your child evaluate how well the plan is providing the results they are after. Help them focus on reasonable expectations, looking for progress rather than perfection. Some kids will only feel redeemed from past strikeouts by hitting the next ball out of the park. All they need to do for now is raise their batting average. You can refocus your child by asking how their current performance compares to what was happening before the current plan.

They may decide that with more time the current plan will deliver the desired results, or they may see the need to tweak part of it. For instance, your child may need to change the time of day they perform a particular step, the order of one or two steps in a process, or the type and timing of rewards. Sometimes a strategy will stop being effective because some aspect of your child's life has changed. A new schedule, a new teacher, a new subject at school, or a new level of hormones can render a strategy ineffective. When this happens you know what to do. Go back to the drawing board and brainstorm on new strategies and repeat the planning process.

If nothing in the plan seems to be working or the plan never gets off the ground, it may indicate that something in the plan didn't match something in reality. That's okay. Nothing lost. You and your child might have just gained some essential insight that is key to their success in life. Here are a few questions to bring that insight to light:

- Does their goal take them where they really want to go?
  Persistence requires at least a portion of passion.

- Do they have confidence and belief that they can reach their goal?
  Action is always based on belief.

- Does the plan leverage what they like?
  The pursuit of pleasure often makes a perfect copilot.

- Does the measure for success match reasonable expectations?
  When standing at the foot of a mountain, it is the only place we can start our climb.

- Do the strategies leverage their superpowers or rely on their deficiencies?
  Eagles should fly, cheetahs should run, and giraffes should eat leaves.

- Are unexpressed or unrecognized emotional blocks keeping them from taking certain steps?
  Whatever we fear the most will determine our outcome.

That last question may be one that neither you nor your child can answer. However, if they have a genuine desire toward the end goal but seem to be paralyzed at the starting line, the culprit may be emotional scars or deep-seated fears that neither of you are aware of. If you suspect that to be true, seek out a therapist trained to identify and deal with powerful emotions tied to their perceptions of past experiences. Remember that memories are made up of incomplete pictures and the thoughts and emotions attached to them. A trained therapist can help your child reframe their pictures so that their thoughts about it change and their emotions become less potent and less disabling. Some blocks can be removed in a short amount of time; others may be more persistent. Either way the sooner you start the sooner your child can get back to pursuing their individual flavor of a fulfilling life.

Regardless of the results or where you have to go back to, each attempt is forward progress. Each step backward can be a step forward. That is a strange concept for most of us humans; nevertheless, it is quite true. Hindsight really is 20/20, and there is only one way to gain hindsight.

Continue to repeat this cycle of brainstorming, planning, working, and evaluating until you implement a strategy that fits and that strategy becomes part of your child's more empowered future. The most valuable result for them will not be reaching their goal; it will be learning how to reach any goal they set in life.

AN ADD COACH CAN HELP

For any number of reasons, keeping your child moving in a positive direction may require getting help. Perhaps your own ADD symptoms are getting in the way of helping them get organized and execute a plan. You may simply lack the time or energy at this stage in your life, career, or situation. Especially if you are a single parent, both your time and energy are likely to be spread thin. Perhaps you are too close to the situation to approach it objectively or your relationship with your child still carries too much emotional baggage. That's okay; some such issues require time to reach their evolutionary resolution.

An ADD coach can provide the help you need. They are not only experts at facilitating self-learning and achievement, they are also knowledgeable on how the ADD brain works and techniques to acti-

> For any number of reasons, keeping your child moving
> in a positive direction may require getting help.

vate it. A coach can help you help your child or work directly with them under your supervision. If your child is older, a coach may need to work with them independently while you take on the supportive role of cheerleader. Being familiar with the process of forward motion will help you select the right coach and understand the patient process they will pursue.

If you decide to enlist the help of an ADD coach to accelerate your child's success, be sure to find someone who has been properly trained. You can find links to ADD coaches' organizations at www.ADDParentingSupport.com.

Some Final
Encouragement

I know that your child is an amazing person in spite of what others may think of them or what they may think of themselves. You know that in your heart better than I do. You've seen the small things they do that are evidence of their noble qualities and great potential. I know that you are doing everything you can to help them obtain the success and happiness they deserve.

ONE STEP AT A TIME

You may feel overwhelmed at this point in this book. Relax, take three deep breaths, and clear your mind of everything you just learned. Then start at the beginning of the book and work on step one, *Understanding ADD*. That doesn't mean you won't be working on the other steps. Remember, your subconscious mind will be sorting out those steps both day and night. Trust it to do its job.

When you feel somewhat comfortable with your understanding of ADD and its challenges, reread step two, *Accepting Your Child.* You will want to continue the first step of learning and understanding, but you can't get stuck there. Before too long you will know it is time to jump into step two. When you do, you will probably notice that it is almost done. Focus on the remaining issues that you have to accept about the situation you and your child are in. If you are still too emotional about some aspects of it, I suggest you do some journaling. Writing is a good way to let your subconscious mind speak to you and help you discharge your emotions. Continue to write every day or two until you feel no emotions, good or bad, about the issues you are dealing with, until there is no judgment. Even a positive emotion can indicate that you are trying to compensate for a fear or concern. The only positive emotion left should be your love for your child.

Once you feel at peace with what you are up against, you are ready to put more intentional effort into step three, *Empathizing with Your Child.* Start looking at situations through your child's eyes. You may be a natural at this or it may take lots of practice. Keep at it until you can interact with your son or daughter with understanding and compassion, instead of judgment and criticism.

IF YOU HAVE ADD

If you have ADD, you are lucky. All of the important steps you are taking to prepare to help your child will also prepare you to help yourself. You will start to understand and accept your own challenges in life. You will think back on painful experiences or failures in your own life and understand what was really happening. Tell yourself and those who were there with you that you were all doing the best you could, based on your nature and the knowledge you had at the time. Work to change your recordings of past experiences so that they don't hold you back in the present any longer. Treat yourself with more compassion the next time you make a mistake. Talk about yourself in more accurate terms, instead of beating yourself up each time you disappoint yourself or others. If you catch your critic saying something that doesn't support your success, stop him mid-sentence with a snap on the wrist with a rubber band or a defiant, "Shut your big head up!"

If you have ADD, some steps in helping your child will be easier and some will be harder. The one step that is the hardest for most people, empathizing, will come naturally for you. Being consistent at implementing strategies will likely be harder. That's okay. Simply do the things you are good at and get help from others to do the rest. If you are struggling, delegate some tasks to your spouse, rely on a close friend, or get help from a trained ADD coach. Some coaches specialize in both childhood and adult ADD and can help both of you.

MOTIVATE YOURSELF

As you are working hard to motivate your son or daughter, don't forget about yourself. Parenting can be discouraging, especially if your child has ADD. You have to set yourself up to get through the tough times—the times when nothing you do seems to matter; when your child is taking those necessary steps backward; when you are worn out and feel unappreciated.

The concept of visualization can help get you through those times and keep you learning and working at it the best way you know how. Below is an exercise in visualization that will help you keep the end in mind.

Sit down and write a future letter from your child to you. Have your child tell you how well he is doing. Have them thank you for learning about ADD and helping them understand themselves. Have them say that they know raising them was not easy, but that they are grateful for all your patience and understanding, for never giving up on them and believing they would make it. Then, have them tell you that they hope they do as good of a job raising the baby that just came into their life as you did raising them. Finally, have them express to you their pure and simple love for you. Don't just copy my words. Personalize it to fit your situation. Include those things you would love to hear.

> Learning plus effort always equals progress, and progress
> is more powerful than perfection. Perfection is a myth
> that we can never achieve, but progress gives us hope
> and tells us we are moving in the right direction.

I happen to know after having raised six kids that sooner or later a letter or card with those sentiments will come. Having been a very challenging child, I know that my own mother loved me and worked hard and did her best with what she had and what she knew at the time. If you just keep learning and doing your best, sooner or later your child will realize how much you blessed their life.

The problem is, you won't need that letter then as much as you do now, so write it now and take it out whenever you get discouraged and read it to yourself.

BE PATIENT

My final advice to you is to be patient with yourself. You are going to slip up at times and become part of the problem, instead of part of the solution. Simply apologize and ask for your child's forgiveness, just like I have so many times. A sincere apology will help return your relationship to one of trust and cooperation. It will also boost their self-esteem much more than you pretending to be a perfect parent.

As I constantly preached to the kids I've coached in basketball, "Do your best and your best gets better." Keep learning and keep trying. Learning plus effort always equals progress, and progress is more powerful than perfection. Perfection is a myth that we can never achieve, but progress gives us hope and tells us we are moving in the right direction; just like you are now.

ABOUT THE AUTHOR

Sterling Pratt grew up with a debilitating dose of ADD and SAD. He has supported his family for the last thirty years working with large

 corporate computer systems. He and his wife, Terry, fell in love at first sight in 1974. Since then they have worked together to raise six children, some of which are ADD, SAD and OCD. As part of that parenting effort Sterling has gained experience working with youth as a Scout Master, youth leader, and basketball and soccer coach. He has recorded his often bizarre experiences growing up with undiagnosed ADD in a separate book that will be released next year, called *Pudd'nhead Adventures*.

BUY A SHARE OF THE FUTURE IN YOUR COMMUNITY

These certificates make great holiday, graduation and birthday gifts that can be personalized with the recipient's name. The cost of one S.H.A.R.E. or one square foot is $54.17. The personalized certificate is suitable for framing and will state the number of shares purchased and the amount of each share, as well as the recipient's name. The home that you participate in "building" will last for many years and will continue to grow in value.

THIS CERTIFIES THAT

YOUR NAME HERE

HAS INVESTED IN A HOME FOR A DESERVING FAMILY

1985-2010

TWENTY-FIVE YEARS OF BUILDING FUTURES
IN OUR COMMUNITY ONE HOME AT A TIME

1200 SQUARE FOOT HOUSE @ $65,000 = $54.17 PER SQUARE FOOT
This certificate represents a tax deductible donation. It has no cash value.

Here is a sample SHARE certificate:

YES, I WOULD LIKE TO HELP!

I support the work that Habitat for Humanity does and I want to be part of the excitement! As a donor, I will receive periodic updates on your construction activities but, more importantly, I know my gift will help a family in our community realize the dream of homeownership. **I would like to SHARE in your efforts against substandard housing in my community!** *(Please print below)*

PLEASE SEND ME _____ SHARES at $54.17 EACH = $ $_____

In Honor Of: _____

Occasion: (Circle One)   HOLIDAY   BIRTHDAY   ANNIVERSARY

        OTHER: _____

Address of Recipient: _____

Gift From: _____ *Donor Address:* _____

Donor Email: _____

I AM ENCLOSING A CHECK FOR $ $_____ PAYABLE TO HABITAT FOR HUMANITY <u>OR</u> PLEASE CHARGE MY VISA OR MASTERCARD *(CIRCLE ONE)*

Card Number _____ Expiration Date: _____

Name as it appears on Credit Card _____ Charge Amount $ _____

Signature _____

Billing Address _____

Telephone # Day _____ Eve _____

PLEASE NOTE: Your contribution is tax-deductible to the fullest extent allowed by law.
Habitat for Humanity • P.O. Box 1443 • Newport News, VA 23601 • 757-596-5553
www.HelpHabitatforHumanity.org

Printed in the USA
CPSIA information can be obtained
at www.ICGtesting.com
JSHW022341140824
68134JS00019B/1618

9 781614 481034